COOK IT LIGHT CLASSICS

Jeanne Jones

MACMILLAN · USA

MACMILLAN
A Prentice Hall Macmillan Company
15 Columbus Circle
New York, NY 10023

Library of Congress Cataloging-in-Publication Data

Jones, Jeanne.
    Cook it light classics / Jeanne Jones.
        p.   cm.
    Includes index.
    ISBN 0-02-033901-1 (pbk)
    1. Low-calorie diet—Recipes.   2. Low-fat diet—Recipes.   3. Salt-free diet—Recipes.   I. Title.
    RM222.2.J618   1992
    641.5′63—dc20   92-19255   CIP

Manufactured in the United States of America
10 9 8 7 6 5 4 3 2 1

ACKNOWLEDGMENTS

Tracy DeMas, recipe testing; Bradley J. Chamberlin, manuscript preparation; William Hansen, editorial assistance and nutritional analysis; Justin Schwartz, editorial assistance; Pam Hoenig, editor; Margret McBride, literary agent.

PREFACE

Writing my column, "Cook It Light," syndicated by King Features Syndicate, continues to be as exciting a weekly event for me as it was when I wrote the first *Cook It Light* cookbook in 1987.

What has changed in the five years since that book was published is that I now have over twenty million readers every week. However, the key to my own enjoyment of the column is still the same. I write what is called an interacting column; in other words, my readers write to me, and their letters, along with my answers, appear in my column.

I also still love being referred to as the "Dear Abby" of the food section. The only difference is that my readers don't send me their personal problems—they send me their recipes that need help! Sometimes, rather than sending me a recipe, a reader will ask me for my lighter version of an old-fashioned favorite such as pound cake or tuna noodle casserole.

When a reader does send me a favorite recipe to be revised so it has fewer calories and less cholesterol and sodium, I first make it just as it is written. This way I have the taste, texture, and appearance I need to duplicate in the revision.

Sometimes it's easy and I am able to come very close to the original recipe with a much lighter version in one or two tries. Other times I have to make numerous passes at it before I am satisfied that my light recipe is close enough to the original that any one of you would be happy with the results.

I have received thousands of letters telling me how educational my column is. I want to thank all of you and tell you that my column continues to be an ongoing education for me. I have learned more ways to substitute fresh and natural ingredients for the processed foods found in cans, bottles, boxes, and envelopes than I ever knew existed.

It has been so much fun revising and assembling all the favorite recipes that appear in this book. I have also included a few of my own favorite recipes that I have developed for famous spas, hotels, and restaurants—and some tips on how you can start creating your own "light" recipes.

Enjoy my book—and please continue writing to me. I love your letters and your recipes!

WHY COOK IT LIGHT

L*ight* is both an adjective and a noun. *Light*, the adjective, means "less heavy." *Light*, the noun, is something that illuminates, enlightens, or informs. In this case, "cook it light" means to cook it with less fat for fewer calories; less food of animal origin for lower cholesterol and less saturated fat; less salt and high-sodium ingredients to reduce the amount of sodium consumed. But "cook it light" also means make it imaginative and satisfying. Deprivation *still* has no place in my vocabulary.

Cook It Light could also be called *Cook It Smart*. In fact, the recipes and information contained in this book all reflect and adhere to the guidelines explained in my book, *Eating Smart, The ABC's of the New Food Literacy*. Now, more than ever before, we have been made aware of the importance of proper nutrition for good health. We now know that our health has more to do with what we do for ourselves than what our doctors can do for us. No one else can control how many calories we eat or how much fat, cholesterol, and sodium we consume.

Unfortunately, five years after the first edition of *Cook It Light* was published, there are still people who think food has to be *either* good *or* good for you. Fortunately nothing could be further from the truth. In *Cook It Light* nutrition and the joy of truly fine food are combined to create dishes that are both healthful and delicious. Using the recipes in this book, you can enjoy the international cuisines and the American regional cooking you like best. Using my techniques for lowering the fat, calories, cholesterol, and sodium, you can lighten your own recipes without losing any of the taste, texture, or appearance of your favorite dishes.

COOK-IT-LIGHT MEAL PLANNING

When planning your menus, it is important to consider the overall balance of the meal. For example, you would not want to serve a rich, hearty soup with poultry or meat in it before serving pot roast for the entrée. A crisp, fresh garden salad would be a better choice.

Also remember you want a variety in taste range, color, and texture in your menus. When possible, avoid using the same ingredients in each course. Serving carrot soup with steamed carrots as the vegetable on your entrée plate and carrot cake for dessert will never win an award for exciting menu planning, no matter how good each individual course may be. Nor would a plate with roast chicken, mashed potatoes, and cauliflower create visual excitement. The meal would be far more interesting and visually satisfying if you served new potatoes with their reddish skins intact and broccoli or carrots to add even more color. The combination of texture or "mouth feel" between the ingredients used in any one dish can also add greatly to its appeal. For example, a salad with crisp greens, soft cheese, and crunchy toasted nuts or seeds is much more exciting than a salad with only one texture.

I like to plan my menus around a theme. By putting together

menus that incorporate a national or ethnic theme, the taste ranges will be compatible and you will have more fun planning and preparing the meals. It is such fun to decorate appropriately for a party; even a small family dinner is more fun and more exciting when you turn it into a dining event.

COOK-IT-LIGHT RECIPE REVISION

For my column, "Cook It Light," to revise the recipes sent to me by my readers, I first have to make the recipe exactly as it was sent to me. This gives me a basis for comparison, or what we call the "benchmark." The following chart will show you how I mark a recipe to start the testing process. Fortunately, my job has become a lot easier since the food industry has responded to consumers' increased nutritional awareness by introducing wonderful new fat-and-cholesterol-reduced and fat-and-cholesterol-free products which can be substituted for their higher fat, higher cholesterol counterparts. For the revised version of the following recipe, see page 109.

The recipe contains three problem ingredients that need to be eliminated, reduced, or replaced.

1. *Problem:* What's wrong with the ingredient? Put the problems in the order of importance with your *biggest* concern first.
2. *Function:* What is the purpose of the problem ingredient in the original recipe? Perhaps it can simply be eliminated. List in the order of its perceived importance.
3. *Solution:* What are acceptable substitutes for the problems? You may want to try several possibilities, depending on the desired results (i.e., low-sodium soup or make-your-own).
4. *Results:* How much did you save? This is the payoff—the rewards are plain to see. You really *can* have it all!

RECITE ANALYSIS

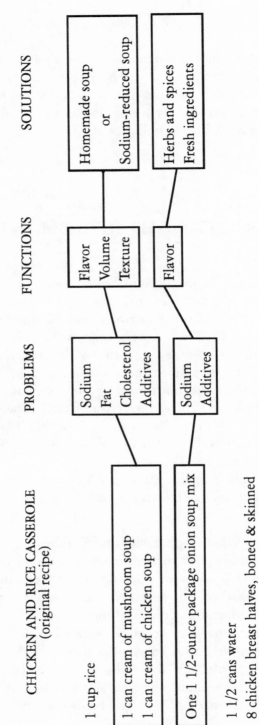

CHICKEN AND RICE CASSEROLE
(original recipe)

PROBLEMS

FUNCTIONS

SOLUTIONS

1 cup rice

1 can cream of mushroom soup
1 can cream of chicken soup

One 1 1/2-ounce package onion soup mix

1 1/2 cans water
8 chicken breast halves, boned & skinned

Sodium
Fat
Cholesterol
Additives

Sodium
Additives

Flavor
Volume
Texture

Flavor

Homemade soup
or
Sodium-reduced soup

Herbs and spices
Fresh ingredients

Original Recipe	*Per Serving*	*Revised Recipe*
275	Total Calories	260
53mg	Cholesterol	50mg
7g	Fat	5g
1,163mg	Sodium	405mg

COOK-IT-LIGHT NUTRITION

The nutrition information at the end of each recipe is derived from software developed by Practorcare, Inc., of San Diego. However, to bring nutritional information into perspective, I like to point out that if you take two oranges of exactly the same size and color, and off the same tree, to a laboratory for analysis, they will not be the same. In other words, nutritional analysis cannot be considered an exact science; at best, it is an educated guess. To do your own nutritional analysis, there are many good references in both print and software form now available. Check your local library, bookstore, or computer software center for resources.

Calories have only four sources—the three food groups, carbohydrates, proteins, and fats—plus alcohol. Carbohydrate foods and protein foods both contain four calories per gram. Fats contain nine calories per gram, or more than twice as many as carbohydrates and proteins; and alcohol contains seven calories per gram—almost twice as many. It is easy to see that if you want to control calories, it is important to greatly reduce your intake of fat and alcohol, since they are the two major sources of calories with the least amount of nutrition.

After each recipe in this book you will find not only the total calories given, but also the milligrams of cholesterol and sodium, and the grams of fat. To find out what percentage of calories are coming from fat in any given recipe, simply multiply the grams of fat by 9 and then divide that number by the total number of calories. Then multiply the answer by 100. For example, in the preceding illustration showing how to revise a recipe, the original recipe contains 7 grams of fat: $7 \times 9 = 63$. Divide 63 (the total fat calories) by 275 (the total calories): $63 \div 275 = .23 \times 100 = 23$ (23 percent of the calories are coming from fat).

Remember that it isn't so important that you worry about every single recipe, but rather the total for the day. If you are allowing yourself 3,000 calories a day, that means you should consume no more than 100 grams of fat per day. That is if you want to stay within the 30 percent or less of the calories consumed coming from fat that is currently recommended by the American Heart Association. This amounts to a little over half a cup of regular margarine or a little less than half a cup of olive oil per day. Wouldn't you think it would be easy to limit fat intake; especially when you consider how unpleasant it would be to eat or drink a half cup of fat? Yet the average American gets about 39 percent of the calories consumed from fat! That's why knowing how to "Cook It Light" is so important.

COOKING TIPS

Cook in nonstick cookware or use a nonstick vegetable spray on your pans and baking dishes to prevent sticking rather than use butter, margarine, or oil.

Use water, defatted stock, juice, or wine instead of butter, margarine, or oil to prevent sticking or burning when sautéeing.

When sautéeing onions, garlic, or shallots for a sauce, cook them, covered, over low heat, adding a little water, stock, or wine to prevent scorching rather than butter, margarine, or oil. This will save you a whopping 120 calories per tablespoon of sautéeing fat omitted from your final dish.

When making salad dressings, it is not necessary to add the classic two parts of oil to a part of vinegar. You can extend dressing with water, adding only 1 to 2 tablespoons of oil per cup, and still have a delicious, flavorful dressing.

To reduce the amount of saturated fat, always buy lean cuts of meat and remove all visible fat. Remove the skin from all poultry.

Use cooking techniques which allow any remaining fat to drip off during the cooking process, such as broiling, roasting on a rack, or poaching. If using pan drippings for gravy, refrigerate them long enough for the fat to congeal on top so that it can be removed. Also, when making stews or soups, use this same method of refrigerating them and removing the fat before reheating and serving.

Avoid products containing coconut oil, palm kernel oil, and solid chocolate. Most nondairy creamers contain coconut oil, so read the labels. For coconut flavor use coconut extract, and for chocolate use powdered cocoa. In place of butter, use a pure corn-oil margarine or vegetable oils high in monounsaturated fat, such as canola oil or olive oil.

To reduce the sodium in your recipes, compensate by increasing the herbs and spices. Always crush your dried herbs before adding them to the other ingredients so they will release their maximum "flavor" (their aroma). Often merely adding a little lemon juice or vinegar will give just the right "lift" to the recipe, without adding any salt.

You can almost always reduce the amount of sugar called for in recipes by one third to one half. Or reduce granulated white sugar (sucrose) by one third simply by substituting fructose, which is one and one half times sweeter.

Substitute unsweetened frozen fruit juice concentrate (undiluted orange, apple, or pineapple) for some of the liquid in the recipe to further reduce the amount of refined sugar, or raise the level of perceived sweetness without adding any sweetener by using vanilla and/or ground cinnamon.

SOUPS AND STOCKS

Making your own stock is the single most important step toward becoming a truly fine cook. Even though now there are some very acceptable frozen and canned stocks to be found in the market, the reasons for making your own still outweigh the convenience of the store-bought varieties, not to mention the money you can save.

I have had so many readers tell me that they don't have time to make their own stock that I finally did a column called "Fifteen-Minute Stock," which I have incorporated into my recipe for chicken stock in this section.

Remember the old cliché, "A watched pot never boils?" This refers to the days when some person in the kitchen was designated to make sure the stock never came to a full boil. When making your own stock, never allow the pot to actually come to a full boil. When it starts to boil, reduce the heat and simmer the stock. This is especially important if you want a clear stock.

Don't add salt or much seasoning so that you can adjust the salt and seasonings for the individual recipe. Almost all of the calories and cholesterol in stock are in the fat, so after defatting your stock you do not have to worry about either one of them. Once you have defatted your stock, freeze it in containers of a volume you most often use. I store my own in ice-cube trays. When the stock is solidly frozen, I remove the cubes from the trays and place them in plastic bags. Two cubes equal about ¼ cup, so measuring is very simple.

After your chicken stock has cooked for an hour or more, you may want to throw in a whole chicken and cook it for your dinner or have it to dice for a salad or casserole the next day. It will take the chicken less than an hour to cook, and overcooking can make it tough and dry; so as soon as it is tender, remove it from the stockpot. A three-pound stewing chicken will yield about three cups chopped cooked meat.

FIFTEEN-MINUTE CHICKEN STOCK

3 to 5 pounds chicken bones, parts, and giblets, excluding the
  liver
2 medium carrots, scraped and chopped
2 celery ribs, without leaves, chopped
1 large onion, unpeeled, quartered
3 parsley sprigs
2 to 4 cloves garlic, unpeeled, halved
1 bay leaf
12 peppercorns
¼ cup vinegar
Cold water to cover by one inch

1. Put all the ingredients into a large pot with a lid. Add cold water to cover and bring slowly to a boil. Preparation to this point takes about 5 minutes.

2. Reduce the heat to low, cover, leaving the lid ajar, and

simmer for 3 hours or more. Longer cooking makes the stock more flavorful. Remove from the heat and allow to stand until cool enough to handle. Remove the chicken parts and vegetables and discard. Strain the stock and cool to room temperature. This second step takes 5 minutes more. Refrigerate, uncovered, overnight or until the fat has congealed on top.

3. Remove the fat and store the stock in the freezer in containers of a volume you most often use. This final step completes the 15 minutes of preparation time.

MAKES ABOUT 10 CUPS

1 cup contains approximately:
Calories / Negligible   Cholesterol / Negligible
Fat / Negligible   Sodium / Varies

BEEF STOCK

Beef stock is made exactly the same way you make chicken stock except you brown the bones and vegetables prior to starting the stock. The reason for browning the ingredients is to give a rich, dark color to the stock. Pale meat stocks do not make sauces and gravies look as rich and appetizing. Also, a foam or scum rises to the surface of a meat stock and must be removed at least once and sometimes several times when the stock first comes to a boil. Veal knuckles are ideal to use for the bones. The optional addition of the beef or veal makes for a richer stock.

3 pounds beef or veal bones
1 pound beef or veal, any cut (optional)
1 medium tomato, halved
3 medium carrots, scraped and chopped
2 celery ribs, without leaves, chopped

1 *large onion, unpeeled, quartered*
3 *parsley sprigs*
3 *cloves garlic, unpeeled, halved*
¼ *teaspoon dried thyme, crushed*
¼ *teaspoon dried marjoram, crushed*
1 *bay leaf*
12 *peppercorns*
¼ *cup vinegar*
Cold water to cover by one inch

1. Place the bones, meat, and vegetables in a roasting pan in a 400°F oven until well browned, about 40 minutes, turning frequently to brown evenly.

2. Remove them from the roasting pan and place in a large pot with a lid. Add all the other ingredients and cover with cold water. Bring slowly to a boil. Simmer slowly for 5 minutes and remove any scum on the surface. Reduce the heat, cover, leaving the lid ajar, and simmer for 2 to 6 hours. Cooking longer makes the stock more flavorful.

3. Remove from the heat and allow to stand until cool enough to handle. Remove the bones, meat, and vegetables and discard. Strain the stock and cool to room temperature.

4. Refrigerate, uncovered, overnight or until the fat has congealed on top. Remove the fat and store the stock in the freezer in the size containers you most often use.

MAKES ABOUT 10 CUPS

1 cup contains approximately:
Calories / Negligible   Cholesterol / Negligible
Fat / Negligible   Sodium / Varies

DRIED ONION SOUP MIX

This soup mix can be used in any recipe that calls for dried onion soup mix. It is much lower in sodium than the commercial mixes and it contains no added preservatives. If you are making it ahead, store it in a tightly covered container in the refrigerator.

½ teaspoon onion powder
½ teaspoon salt
¼ teaspoon sugar
¼ teaspoon Kitchen Bouquet Browning Sauce
½ cup chopped or minced dehydrated onion

Combine the onion powder, salt, and sugar in a small bowl. Add the Kitchen Bouquet and stir until the seasonings are uniformly brown. Add the dehydrated onion and mix thoroughly until the color is again even. (This step takes several minutes.) Makes the equivalent of one 1.5-ounce envelope dried onion soup mix.

MAKES ½ CUP MIX

1 tablespoon mix contains approximately:
Calories / 12   Cholesterol / None
Fat / None   Sodium / 149mg

FRENCH GARDENER'S SOUP

BEANS

½ cup small white beans, soaked overnight and drained (see Note on page 14)
1 medium onion, peeled and stuck with 2 cloves
1 medium carrot, peeled and quartered
½ teaspoon salt

¼ *teaspoon freshly ground black pepper*
½ *teaspoon dried thyme, crushed*
½ *teaspoon dried rosemary, crushed*

VEGETABLES

2 *medium turnips, peeled and cut in 1-inch cubes*
2 *medium potatoes, peeled and cut in 1-inch cubes*
2 *celery ribs, sliced into ¼-inch crescents*
3 *large carrots, peeled and sliced in ½-inch rounds*
4 *leeks, white part only, sliced in ½-inch rounds*
¼ *medium head of cabbage, shredded*
5 *cups water*
1 *teaspoon salt*
¼ *teaspoon freshly ground black pepper*
1 *teaspoon dried thyme, crushed*
1 *teaspoon dried rosemary, crushed*
Finely chopped fresh parsley for garnish (optional)

1. Combine all the bean ingredients, cover with water, and bring to a boil. Reduce the heat to simmer and cook until the beans are tender, about 2 hours. Drain the beans and discard the carrots and onion.

2. While the beans are cooking, combine the turnips, potatoes, celery, carrots, leeks, and cabbage with 1 cup of the water in a large pot or soup kettle. Cook, uncovered, over low heat until the vegetables are tender, about 30 minutes. Do not brown!

3. Add the drained beans to the vegetables. Add the remaining water, the salt, pepper, thyme, and rosemary. Bring to a boil, reduce the heat to low and simmer, covered, for 30 minutes. Remove from the heat and allow to cool slightly. Remove 4 cups of the vegetables and puree. Pour the pureed vegetables back into the stew and mix well. Heat to the desired serving temperature.

4. To serve, ladle 1½ cups soup into a bowl or soup plate. Top with chopped parsley, if desired.

MAKES TWELVE 1½-CUP SERVINGS

Each serving contains approximately:
Calories / 131   Cholesterol / None
Fat / 5g   Sodium / 515mg

NOTE: To shorten the soaking time, bring the beans to a boil with enough water to cover by 2 inches. Remove from the heat, cover, and allow to stand 1 hour to soften. Then, pour out the water and proceed as if the beans have soaked overnight.

WILD RICE SOUP

½ cup wild rice, rinsed well in warm water
3 cups water
1 tablespoon corn-oil margarine
1 medium onion, chopped (1½ cups)
½ pound celery, chopped (1½ cups)
½ pound mushrooms, sliced (3 cups)
4 cups defatted chicken stock, heated to simmering
½ pound cooked skinless turkey, chopped (2 cups)
1 cup low-fat milk
½ teaspoon salt (omit if using salted stock)
⅛ teaspoon freshly ground black pepper

1. Combine the rice and water in a saucepan and bring to a boil. Cover and cook over low heat for 40 to 45 minutes or until the rice is tender. Drain off the excess water.

2. Melt the margarine in a large pot over medium-low heat. Add the onions, celery, and mushrooms. Cook until vegetables are crisp-tender, about 5 minutes. Add water or stock, if necessary, to prevent scorching.

3. In a blender container, combine 1 cup of the cooked rice and 1 cup of the hot stock. Process until completely smooth. Add

to the vegetable mixture along with remaining stock, rice, and the chopped turkey.

4. Cook for 30 minutes over medium heat, stirring often to prevent sticking. Add the milk, salt, and pepper just before serving.

MAKES SIX 1-CUP SERVINGS

Each serving contains approximately:
Calories / 190   Cholesterol / 28mg
Fat / 5g   Sodium / 340mg

LIGHT SHERRIED WILD RICE SOUP

⅔ cup wild rice
2 cups water
1 tablespoon corn-oil margarine
2 medium leeks (include some green), chopped (2 cups)
2 large mushrooms, diced (½ cup)
1 cup unbleached all-purpose flour
4 cups cold defatted chicken stock
4 cups hot defatted chicken stock
¼ teaspoon freshly ground black pepper
½ teaspoon salt (omit if using salted stock)
1 cup canned evaporated skimmed milk
3 tablespoons dry sherry

1. Wash the wild rice thoroughly. Place in a heavy saucepan with the water and bring to a boil over medium-high heat. Reduce heat to low and simmer, covered, about 45 minutes until tender but not mushy. Uncover and fluff with a fork. Simmer an additional 5 minutes; drain excess liquid.

2. In a large skillet over medium heat, melt the margarine. Add the leeks and mushrooms and cook, stirring, until soft, about 3 minutes. Place the flour and the cold stock in a blender container and blend until smooth. Add this mixture and the hot stock to the leeks and mushrooms. Bring to a boil, stirring frequently.

3. Add the rice, pepper, and salt. Heat thoroughly. Stir in the milk and sherry. Heat gently, but do not boil.

MAKES TWELVE 1-CUP SERVINGS

Each serving contains approximately:
Calories / 122   Cholesterol / 1mg
Fat / 1g   Sodium / 138mg

LIGHT PUMPKIN SOUP

This is a wonderful first course for a Halloween dinner party. If you're serving buffet style, you may want to serve the soup in a large hollowed-out pumpkin.

1 small pumpkin (3 to 4 pounds), 6 to 8 cups cubed (see
Note on page 18)
2 tablespoons water
4 celery ribs, chopped (2 cups)
2 medium leeks, white part only, chopped (1 cup)
1 medium onion, chopped (1½ cups)
6 cups defatted chicken stock
½ teaspoon salt (omit if using salted stock)
¼ cup corn-oil margarine
¾ cup unbleached all-purpose flour
1 cup low-fat milk

1. Peel, split in half, and remove the seeds from the pumpkin. Wash the seeds under running cold water to remove pulp. Pat the seeds dry with paper towels, place on a baking sheet and toast in

a preheated 275°F oven for 45 minutes. While the seeds are toasting cut one-fourth of the pumpkin meat into strips 1¼ inches long and ⅛ inch thick. Refrigerate these strips for later use as garnish. Cut the remaining pumpkin meat into 1-inch cubes.

2. Remove the pumpkin seeds from oven and allow them to cool on the baking sheet. When they have cooled, store them in a covered plastic container at room temperature.

3. Heat a small amount of water in a 4-quart sauce pot over medium heat. When hot, add all the chopped vegetables except the pumpkin and cook 5 minutes, adding more water if needed to keep the vegetables from scorching. Add the pumpkin and cook an additional 5 minutes, stirring frequently. Add the stock and salt and bring to a boil. Reduce the heat to low and simmer, covered, until the pumpkin cubes are fork tender, 25 to 30 minutes.

4. Melt the margarine in a 2-quart saucepan over low heat. Add the flour, stirring constantly with a wire whisk and cook 2 to 3 minutes, being careful not to scorch the flour mixture. Strain 4 cups of the simmering stock into the flour mixture and whisk vigorously until smooth. Add this mixture to the vegetables and stock remaining in the 4-quart pot. Whisk until well blended and simmer for 10 minutes more.

5. Remove the soup from the heat. Puree in a food processor (this will need to be done in 2 steps in most processors). Strain and return the soup to the pot. Return the pot to the stove and bring to a simmer.

6. In a small saucepan, combine the milk and pumpkin strips and bring to a simmer over low heat. When hot, add to the soup mixture, stirring until well blended.

7. To serve, spoon the soup into bowls and garnish with toasted pumpkin seeds. Serve immediately.

MAKES EIGHT 1-CUP SERVINGS

Each serving contains approximately:
Calories / 180   Cholesterol / 2mg
Fat / 8g   Sodium / 230mg

NOTE: If pumpkins are unavailable, two 1½- to 2-pound acorn squash may be substituted for an equally delicious soup.

BLACK BEAN SOUP

1 cup (8 ounces) dried black beans, rinsed and picked over
2 cups chopped onion
6 cups vegetable stock or water
2 cups chopped fresh tomatoes (1 pound)
1½ cups seeded and diced green bell pepper
1 cup dried celery
4 cloves garlic, minced
1½ ounces jalapeño pepper, seeded, deveined, and minced
1 tablespoon ground cumin
1 teaspoon dried oregano, crushed
1 bay leaf
1 teaspoon salt (omit if using salted stock)
¼ teaspoon freshly ground black pepper
⅛ teaspoon red pepper flakes
½ cup light sour cream
2 tablespoons chopped fresh cilantro
Chopped fresh cilantro for garnish

1. Soak the beans for at least 8 hours, or overnight. Drain and rinse thoroughly.

2. Cook the onion, covered, in a large, heavy pot over low heat about 15 to 20 minutes, until soft. Stir occasionally and add a little water, if necessary, to prevent scorching. Add the stock and bring to a boil over medium heat. Stir in the beans and cook, covered, for 60 minutes. Remove 1½ cups of the stock and bean mixture, puree, and add back to the pot.

3. Stir in the remaining ingredients except the sour cream and cilantro. Reduce the heat to low and simmer, covered, for 40

minutes. Remove the cover, stir in the cilantro and cook an additional 25 minutes. Remove the bay leaf and adjust the seasonings, if needed.

4. To serve, ladle 1 cup of soup into each of eight soup bowls. Top with 1 tablespoon sour cream and a sprinkling of chopped cilantro.

MAKES EIGHT 1-CUP SERVINGS

Each serving contains approximately:
Calories / 155   Cholesterol / 6mg
Fat / 3g   Sodium / 400mg

SOUTHWESTERN CORN CONSOMME

2 corn tortillas, cut into ¼-inch strips
4 cups defatted chicken stock
1 cup chopped onion
2 cups peeled, chopped fresh tomatoes
½ teaspoon salt (omit if using salted stock)
⅛ teaspoon cayenne pepper
1 teaspoon ground cumin
1 teaspoon chili powder
1 bay leaf, broken
1½ cups fresh corn kernels or 1½ cups frozen, thawed

1. Preheat the oven to 400°F. Spread the tortilla strips evenly on an ungreased baking sheet. Bake, stirring occasionally, until crisp and lightly browned, about 10 minutes. Set aside.

2. Combine 1 cup of the stock and the onion in a blender and process on high speed until pureed. Pour the puree into a large pot or soup kettle; do not wash the blender jar. Combine the chopped tomatoes and another cup of the stock in the blender and process on high speed until pureed. Add the tomato puree to

the pot with the onion mixture. Stir in the remaining 2 cups of stock, the salt, cayenne pepper, cumin, chili powder, and bay leaf. Mix well and slowly bring to a boil over medium heat. Reduce heat to low and simmer, uncovered, for 25 minutes.

3. Remove the soup from the heat and pour through a strainer. Stir the mixture in the strainer so that only a dry pulp remains. Press any remaining liquid in the pulp through the strainer with the back of a spoon. Return the soup to the pot, add the corn and simmer over medium-low heat, uncovered, until the soup is heated through, about 5 minutes.

4. To serve, ladle 1 cup of soup into each of six bowls. Top each serving with toasted tortilla strips.

MAKES SIX 1-CUP SERVINGS

Each serving contains approximately:
Calories / 100   Cholesterol / None
Fat / 2g   Sodium / 283mg

SWISS VEGETABLE BISQUE

1 tablespoon corn-oil margarine
3 tablespoons unbleached all-purpose flour
4 cups defatted chicken stock
½ pound coarsely chopped broccoli (2 cups)
¾ cup chopped carrots
½ cup chopped celery
1 small clove garlic, minced
¼ teaspoon dried thyme, crushed
¼ teaspoon salt (omit if using salted stock)
⅛ teaspoon freshly ground black pepper
1 cup canned evaporated skimmed milk
1 large egg white
4 ounces reduced-fat Swiss cheese, shredded (1 cup)

1. In a large, heavy pan over low heat, melt the margarine. Add the flour and cook several minutes, stirring constantly. Remove from the heat and slowly stir in the stock. Return to heat and bring to a boil, stirring constantly.

2. To the boiling stock mixture, add the broccoli, carrots, celery, garlic, thyme, salt, and pepper. Simmer 8 minutes, until the vegetables are tender.

3. Mix the milk and egg white together in a small bowl with a wire whisk. Slowly mix in several tablespoons of the soup. Gradually pour the milk mixture into the soup, stirring constantly. Simmer for 10 minutes until thickened. Gradually stir in the cheese and serve immediately.

MAKES SIX 1-CUP SERVINGS

Each serving contains approximately:
Calories / 140   Cholesterol / 12mg
Fat / 5g   Sodium / 271mg

CHEESE SOUP

3 *cups peeled and chopped potatoes*
½ *cup finely diced celery*
½ *cup finely diced carrots*
¼ *cup chopped onion*
1 *tablespoon finely chopped fresh parsley*
1 *cup defatted chicken stock*
½ *teaspoon salt (omit if using salted stock)*
Dash of freshly ground black pepper
1½ *cups nonfat milk*
2 *tablespoons unbleached all-purpose flour*
6 *ounces reduced-fat Cheddar cheese, grated*

1. In a large saucepan, combine the potatoes, celery, carrots, onion, parsley, stock, salt, and pepper. Cover and simmer over low heat until tender, 15 to 20 minutes.

2. Gradually add the milk to the flour and mix well. Pour the milk mixture into the vegetables and cook, stirring constantly, until thickened. Add the grated cheese and stir until the cheese is melted.

MAKES FIVE 1-CUP SERVINGS

Each serving contains approximately:
Calories / 242   Cholesterol / 30mg
Fat / 9g   Sodium / 248mg

DAIRY-FREE CHEDDAR ASPARAGUS SOUP

2 tablespoons corn-oil margarine
½ medium onion, finely chopped (¾ cup)
3 celery ribs, finely chopped (¾ cup)
½ cup unbleached all-purpose flour
6 cups defatted chicken stock, heated to boiling
½ teaspoon crumbled bay leaf (be sure to remove and discard the center spine)
Pinch dry mustard
Dash Tabasco sauce
⅛ teaspoon freshly ground black pepper
⅛ teaspoon Worcestershire sauce
1 pound fresh asparagus, tough ends removed and cut in ½-inch pieces (2 cups)
¼ cup sherry
8 ounces Cheddar-flavored soy or tofu cheese, grated
2 teaspoons minced fresh parsley
Chopped fresh parsley, for garnish

1. Melt the margarine in a heavy pot over medium heat. Add the onion and celery and cook, stirring frequently, until tender but not browned, about 5 minutes.

2. Reduce the heat to low, add the flour and cook, stirring frequently, for about 3 minutes. Do not brown.

3. Add the boiling chicken stock, the bay leaf, the mustard, the Tabasco sauce, the pepper, and the Worcestershire sauce and bring to a boil over medium-high heat. Reduce the heat to medium-low and simmer, uncovered, for 20 minutes.

4. Add the asparagus and continue to cook until tender, about 10 minutes. Stir in the sherry, cheese, and minced parsley and cook and stir with a wire whisk until the cheese is completely blended into the soup, about 5 minutes more. Ladle the soup into heated bowls and sprinkle the top with parsley, if desired. Serve immediately.

MAKES SEVEN 1-CUP SERVINGS

Each serving contains approximately:
Calories / 197   Cholesterol / None
Fat / 9g   Sodium / 318mg

CHILLED MELON SOUP

One 2-pound ripe cantaloupe, peeled, seeded, and chopped (4
   cups)
1 tablespoon fresh lemon juice
1 teaspoon sugar

1. Combine all the ingredients in a blender and process until smooth. Chill thoroughly.

2. Before serving, shake or stir the soup because it will separate when allowed to stand. Serve cold.

MAKES TWO ½-CUP SERVINGS

Each serving contains approximately:
Calories / 60   Cholesterol / None
Fat / Negligible   Sodium / 15mg

SAUCES AND SALAD DRESSINGS

Making rich-tasting, creamy-textured sauces without the added butter and other fats always associated with rich sauces is really easy once you learn the tricks. Reduction is the key.

Reducing a sauce in volume to intensify the flavor or thicken the texture is simply a matter of cooking it longer, uncovered, to reduce the volume—it just boils away. If a recipe tells you to reduce by one half, you literally boil the liquid away until you are left with only half as much as you started with. I often use this technique to intensify flavor and then pour the sauce into a blender in order to get the creamy texture I want. For an even smoother sauce, pour the pureed mixture into a sieve or strainer and press it through using the back of a spoon.

When adding oil for "mouth feel," such as in a tofu sauce, use an oil without a distinct flavor such as canola oil. If you want flavor, however, use the most flavorful oil you can buy such as extra virgin olive oil for an Italian taste or dark sesame oil for Pacific rim–inspired dishes. Stronger flavor means you don't need to use as much of it to achieve the desired results. Always store oils tightly covered in a cool place. Making your own salad dressings takes very little time and can save you an enormous amount of money.

TUSCAN FRESH TOMATO AND BASIL SAUCE

A trick I learned in Italy is to freeze vine-ripened tomatoes when they are at their peak so that you will have truly flavorful tomatoes all year round. Then to peel them just put them in warm tap water and they literally pop right out of their skins! If using fresh tomatoes, plunge them into boiling water for 10 seconds to remove their skins.

2 pounds ripe tomatoes, peeled and diced
½ teaspoon salt
2 cloves garlic, minced, or to taste
½ cup chopped fresh basil
½ cup chopped fresh parsley
2 tablespoons extra virgin olive oil
¼ teaspoon freshly ground black pepper to taste
¼ teaspoon dried red pepper flakes or to taste

1. Sprinkle the tomatoes with the salt and mix well. Place the salted tomatoes in a colander and allow to drain for at least 2 hours.

2. Combine the garlic, basil, parsley, olive oil, and black and red pepper in a large bowl. Add the drained tomatoes and mix well.

MAKES 3 CUPS

½ cup contains approximately:
Calories / 67   Cholesterol / None
Fat / 5g   Sodium / 197mg

CREAMY TOMATO SAUCE

1 tablespoon extra virgin olive oil
4 large, ripe tomatoes (2 pounds), peeled, seeded, and diced
1 tablespoon finely chopped fresh tarragon or 1 teaspoon
   dried, crushed
1 teaspoon finely chopped fresh thyme or ½ teaspoon dried,
   crushed
2 tablespoons rice wine vinegar
2 tablespoons white wine vinegar
1 tablespoon finely chopped shallots
¼ cup canned evaporated skimmed milk
¼ cup sour cream
2 tablespoons unsalted corn-oil margarine

1. Heat the olive oil over medium heat. Add the tomatoes and cook, stirring, until thick, about 15 minutes. Add the tarragon and thyme, mix well, and set aside.

2. Heat the vinegars in a small saucepan over medium-low heat. Add the shallots and cook, stirring, until the liquid is nearly gone. Add the milk and sour cream and stir constantly until reduced by one half. Add the margarine and continue stirring until blended. Add to the tomato sauce and mix well.

MAKES 2½ CUPS

¼ cup contains approximately:
Calories / 85   Cholesterol / 3mg
Fat / 5g   Sodium / 25mg

SIMPLE HOLLANDAISE SAUCE

1 tablespoon arrowroot
½ cup cold water
¾ cup reduced-calorie mayonnaise
¼ cup corn-oil margarine
2 teaspoons fresh lemon juice

1. In a small saucepan, combine the arrowroot and water and mix until completely dissolved. Cook over medium heat until the mixture comes to a boil, stirring constantly until it is clear and thickened. Remove from the heat and set aside.

2. Place the mayonnaise in an ovenproof casserole. Add the margarine and lemon juice. Place in a 300°F oven until the margarine melts, about 5 minutes.

3. Remove from the oven and beat with a wire whisk. Add the reserved arrowroot mixture and continue beating with a wire whisk until smooth.

MAKES 1½ CUPS

2 tablespoons contain approximately:
Calories / 82   Cholesterol / 5mg
Fat / 9g   Sodium / 141mg

HERBED MERLOT SAUCE

1 medium onion, finely chopped (1½ cups)
½ cup Merlot (or any other dry red wine)
1½ cups defatted chicken stock
¼ teaspoon salt (omit if using salted stock)
¼ teaspoon freshly ground black pepper
¼ teaspoon dried thyme, crushed

⅛ *teaspoon dried rosemary, crushed*
¼ *teaspoon fresh lemon juice*

1. Combine the onion and wine in a heavy suacepan. Cook, uncovered, over medium heat until almost dry. Add the stock, salt, pepper, thyme, and rosemary and continue to cook, uncovered, until almost dry again, about 15 to 20 minutes.

2. Spoon the mixture into a blender container, add the lemon juice and process until smooth. Pour through a strainer, pressing the liquid through with the back of a spoon.

MAKES ABOUT ½ CUP

2 tablespoons contain approximately:
Calories / 32   Cholesterol / None
Fat / Negligible   Sodium / 31mg

FRESH CORN COULIS

2 Roma or plum tomatoes, peeled and finely diced
½ *teaspoon salt*
1 tablespoon canola oil
½ *medium onion, finely chopped (¾ cup)*
2 cups fresh or frozen corn kernels
1 cup defatted chicken stock
¼ *teaspoon freshly ground black pepper*
¼ *teaspoon ground cumin*

1. Put the tomatoes in a colander, add the salt and mix well. Allow to drain for at least 1 hour.

2. Heat the oil in a saucepan over medium heat. Add the onion and cook until soft, about 5 minutes. Do not brown. Add the corn and cook 5 minutes more, stirring frequently.

3. Add the stock, pepper, and cumin and bring to a boil. Reduce the heat and simmer, uncovered, 15 minutes. Remove from the heat and cool slightly.

4. When cool enough to handle safely, pour the mixture into a blender container and process on high until smooth. Strain the mixture to remove any pulp and thoroughly wash the blender container.

5. Combine the strained corn mixture and the tomatoes and again process in the blender until completely smooth.

MAKES 1⅔ CUPS

⅓ cup contains approximately:
Calories / 99   Cholesterol / None
Fat / 4g   Sodium / 249mg

RAPID RED PEPPER SAUCE

1 tablespoon extra virgin olive oil
⅓ medium onion, finely chopped (½ cup)
2 medium red bell peppers (½ pound), seeded and chopped (2 cups)
¼ teaspoon salt (omit if using salted stock)
¼ teaspoon freshly ground black pepper
1 cup defatted chicken stock

1. Heat the oil in a saucepan. Add the onion and cook over medium heat, stirring, until soft, about 5 minutes; do not brown. Add the red peppers, salt, and pepper, and cook, stirring, 5 more minutes.

2. Add the stock and bring to a boil. Reduce the heat to low and simmer, uncovered, for 15 minutes. Pour into a blender and puree.

3. Return the sauce to the saucepan and simmer until slightly thickened, about 15 minutes.

MAKES 1½ CUPS

¼ cup contains approximately:
Calories / 39   Cholesterol / Negligible
Fat / 3g   Sodium / 106mg

DOUBLE BERRY SAUCE

2 cups fresh cranberries
½ cup frozen unsweetened apple juice concentrate, thawed
1 tablespoon sugar
½ cup dry red wine
10 fresh or frozen strawberries, sliced
2 small oranges (12 ounces), thinly sliced

1. Combine the cranberries, concentrate, sugar, and wine in a large saucepan. Bring to a boil, then cook gently, uncovered, over low heat for 4 minutes.

2. Remove from the heat and immediately add the strawberries. If using frozen, stir until they are defrosted. Add the oranges, then store the sauce, covered, in the refrigerator. It will keep about 3 to 5 days.

MAKES 2 CUPS

2 tablespoons contain approximately:
Calories / 34   Cholesterol / None
Fat / Negligible   Sodium / 3mg

FRESH CRANBERRY RELISH

2 small oranges
⅔ cup sugar
4 cups fresh cranberries (1 pound)

1.   Wash the oranges well and grate 2 tablespoons of orange peel. Peel the oranges and cut them in pieces, removing the seeds and connecting membranes. Place the oranges in a blender with the grated peel and sugar and mix well.

2.   Using quick pulse motions to preserve the texture, add the cranberries, a few at a time, until all of the berries have been coarsely blended into the relish. (This is best if made several days before you plan to serve it.)

MAKES 4 CUPS

½ cup contains approximately:
Calories / 96   Cholesterol / None
Fat / Negligible   Sodium / 1mg

CHUTNEY SAUCE OR DRESSING

¾ cup crumbled silken tofu (6 ounces)
1 tablespoon sugar
1½ teaspoons curry powder
⅛ teaspoon ground ginger
1 tablespoon fresh lemon juice
2 tablespoons reduced-sodium soy sauce
¼ cup prepared chutney

Combine all the ingredients except the chutney in a blender and process on high until smooth. Pour the mixture into a small bowl, add the chutney and mix well.

MAKES 1 CUP

2 tablespoons contain approximately:
Calories / 50   Cholesterol / None
Fat / 2g   Sodium / 61mg

ALL-PURPOSE SPICY BEANS

One 15-ounce can pinto beans, drained, reserving 2
   tablespoons liquid
1/4 teaspoon salt
1/4 teaspoon freshly ground black pepper
1/4 teaspoon ground cumin
1 teaspoon chili powder
2 drops Tabasco sauce or to taste
1/2 medium onion, minced
1 clove garlic, minced or pressed
One 4-ounce can chopped green chilies, drained

1. Combine the beans, reserved liquid, salt, pepper, cumin, chili powder, and Tabasco in a blender and puree.

2. In a skillet or saucepan over low heat, cook the onions and garlic, covered, until soft, adding a little water if necessary to prevent scorching. Uncover and continue cooking until lightly browned. Stir in the chilies and cook for 3 more minutes. Add the pureed bean mixture and mix well. Heat to desired temperature.

MAKES ABOUT 1 CUP

2 tablespoons contain approximately:
Calories / 50   Cholesterol / None
Fat / Negligible   Sodium / 312mg

MEXICAN SALSA

When working with hot peppers, be sure never to touch your face or eyes. If your skin is sensitive, wearing rubber gloves is recommended.

3 medium, ripe tomatoes, finely diced (2 cups)
½ medium onion, finely diced (¾ cup)
2 tablespoons finely chopped cilantro
½ jalapeño pepper, seeded and finely chopped, or to taste
½ clove garlic, finely chopped, or to taste
¾ teaspoon ground cumin
¾ teaspoon dried oregano, crushed
⅛ teaspoon salt
1 tablespoon fresh lemon juice
1 tablespoon fresh lime juice

Combine all the ingredients, cover, and refrigerate for at least 2 hours before serving.

MAKES 1½ CUPS

¼ cup contains approximately:
Calories / 15   Cholesterol / None
Fat / Negligible   Sodium / 40mg

LIGHT AIOLI

1 cup (8 ounces) silken firm tofu
2 tablespoons fresh lemon juice
2 tablespoons extra virgin olive oil
1 tablespoon minced garlic (3 large cloves)
½ teaspoon salt
⅛ teaspoon freshly ground black pepper

Combine all the ingredients in a blender container and process on high until satin smooth.

MAKES 1 CUP

2 tablespoons contain approximately:
Calories / 54   Cholesterol / None
Fat / 5g   Sodium / 150mg

HERBED MUSTARD SAUCE

2 cups silken soft tofu
2 tablespoons fresh lemon juice
2 tablespoons Dijon mustard
¼ teaspoon chopped fresh thyme
⅛ teaspoon fresh rosemary leaves
1 teaspoon chopped garlic
1 tablespoon extra virgin olive oil
½ cup water
½ teaspoon salt
⅛ teaspoon freshly ground black pepper

Combine all the ingredients in a blender and process until satin smooth.

MAKES 2⅓ CUPS

2 tablespoons contain approximately:
Calories / 27   Cholesterol / None
Fat / 2g   Sodium / 82mg

DILL-LIGHT DIP

1 cup (8 ounces) silken tofu, cubed
1 tablespoon corn oil
1 tablespoon fresh lemon juice
¼ teaspoon salt
1 cup light sour cream
2 tablespoons grated onion
2 tablespoons finely chopped fresh parsley
1½ teaspoons dried dill weed
1½ teaspoons Beau Monde seasoning

1. Place the tofu, corn oil, lemon juice, and salt in a blender and process on high until smooth.

2. Combine with the remaining ingredients and refrigerate overnight in a tightly covered container.

MAKES 2 CUPS

¼ cup contains approximately:
Calories / 80   Cholesterol / 12mg
Fat / 7g   Sodium / 88mg

SMOKED SALMON DIP

1 pound part-skim ricotta cheese
¼ cup plain nonfat yogurt
⅛ teaspoon salt
4 ounces smoked salmon, chopped

1. Combine the ricotta, yogurt, and salt in a blender or food processor and blend until satin smooth.

2. Fold in the smoked salmon. Refrigerate in a covered container for several hours or overnight to blend the flavors. Serve with miniature bagels.

MAKES ABOUT 2 CUPS

2 tablespoons contain approximately:
Calories / 60   Cholesterol / 12mg
Fat / 4g   Sodium / 30mg

LIGHT SPINACH DIP

4 small bunches fresh spinach (2 pounds), well washed, stems
*   removed and chopped, or two 10-ounce packages frozen*
*   chopped spinach, thawed*
6 tablespoons dehydrated minced or chopped onion
3 tablespoons unbleached all-purpose flour
1 tablespoon instant nonfat dry milk
½ teaspoon onion powder
½ teaspoon sugar
¼ teaspoon turmeric
½ teaspoon salt
3 scallions, chopped (⅔ cup)
One 8-ounce can sliced water chestnuts, drained and chopped
1½ cups light sour cream
1 cup reduced-calorie mayonnaise

1. If using fresh spinach, steam it over rapidly boiling water 1 to 2 minutes, until tender, then drain well. If using frozen, simply squeeze out the excess moisture but do not cook.

2. In a small bowl, combine the dehydrated onion, flour, dry milk, onion powder, sugar, turmeric, and salt. In a medium-size bowl, combine the remaining ingredients with the drained spinach.

3. Add the dry ingredients to the spinach mixture and mix well. Chill for several hours. Serve in a hollowed-out bread round, if desired.

MAKES ABOUT 6 CUPS

¼ cup contains approximately:
Calories / 67   Cholesterol / 9mg
Fat / 5g   Sodium / 133mg

LIGHT RANCH DRESSING MIX

¼ cup dried parsley
3 tablespoons dried minced onion
2 teaspoons dried chives
1 teaspoon salt
½ teaspoon garlic powder
½ teaspoon ground celery seed
¼ teaspoon freshly ground black pepper

¼ cup reduced-calorie mayonnaise
¾ cup buttermilk

1. Combine the first seven ingredients in a small jar and mix well. Store in a cool, dry place (makes ½ cup of mix).

2. To make dressing, combine 1 tablespoon of the dressing mix with the mayonnaise and mix thoroughly using a wire whisk. Slowly add the buttermilk, stirring constantly until well mixed. Refrigerate in a tightly covered container.

MAKES 1 CUP OF DRESSING

2 tablespoons contain approximately:
Calories / 20   Cholesterol / 1mg
Fat / 1g   Sodium / 50mg

CREAMY SALAD DRESSING

6 tablespoons plain nonfat yogurt
1 tablespoon reduced-calorie mayonnaise
2 teaspoons fresh lemon juice
2 teaspoons sweet hot mustard
1 teaspoon finely chopped fresh parsley
½ teaspoon Worcestershire sauce
½ teaspoon red wine vinegar
1 small clove garlic, finely chopped (½ teaspoon)
⅛ teaspoon onion powder
½ teaspoon reduced-sodium soy sauce
Pinch freshly ground black pepper and salt

Combine all the ingredients in a small bowl and mix well with a wire whisk. Refrigerate overnight in a tightly covered container.

MAKES ½ CUP

2 tablespoons contain approximately:
Calories / 28   Cholesterol / 2mg
Fat / 1g   Sodium / 137mg

NEW-AGE FRENCH DRESSING

2 tablespoons canola oil
2 tablespoons cider vinegar
2 tablespoons water
⅓ cup unsweetened frozen apple juice concentrate, thawed
½ cup ketchup
Juice of 1 lemon
¼ teaspoon salt
¼ teaspoon freshly ground black pepper
¼ teaspoon paprika
2 teaspoons dried minced onion
⅛ teaspoon garlic powder

Place all the ingredients in pint-size jar and shake until well blended. Store, tightly covered, in the refrigerator. Shake well before each use.

MAKES 1⅓ CUPS

1 tablespoon contains approximately:
Calories / 27   Cholesterol / None
Fat / 1g   Sodium / 98mg

LIME AND GINGER DRESSING

¼ *cup rice wine vinegar*
¼ *teaspoon salt*
1 *tablespoon honey*
½ *teaspoon peeled and grated fresh ginger root*
2 *tablespoons fresh lime juice*
⅛ *teaspoon freshly ground black pepper*
Pinch of cayenne pepper to taste

1. Combine the vinegar and salt and stir until the salt has completely dissolved. Add the honey and stir until thoroughly mixed.

2. Add all the remaining ingredients and mix well. Store, covered, in the refrigerator.

MAKES ABOUT ½ CUP

2 tablespoons contain approximately:
Calories / 20   Cholesterol / None
Fat / None   Sodium / 150mg

SUPER SALAD DRESSING

This is a recipe I revised for the California Egg Commission. It was originally made with raw egg yolks and I turned it into a cooked dressing. Amazingly enough, I really think it is a tastier dressing when cooked.

⅔ *cup teriyaki sauce*
½ *cup fresh lemon juice*
¼ *cup white vinegar*
5 *teaspoons paprika*
2 *teaspoons salt*
3 *large egg yolks, lightly beaten*
2¼ *cups canola oil*
¼ *cup extra virgin olive oil*

1. In a heavy saucepan combine the teriyaki sauce, lemon juice, vinegar, paprika, salt, and egg yolks. Mix thoroughly using a wire whisk. Bring to a simmer over low heat and simmer for 5 minutes, stirring frequently with a whisk. Remove from the heat and allow to cool slightly.

2. Pour the cooled mixture into a blender and turn on at low speed. Slowly pour in the oil, blending thoroughly. Store, tightly covered, in the refrigerator.

MAKES 1 QUART

2 tablespoons contain approximately:
Calories / 165   Cholesterol / 20mg
Fat / 18g   Sodium / 382mg

LOW-CAL LINCOLN HIGHWAY INN DRESSING

One 8-ounce can tomato sauce
1 cup unsweetened frozen apple juice concentrate
6 tablespoons cider vinegar
1 medium onion, chopped
1 teaspoon salt
1 scant teaspoon freshly ground black pepper
1 scant teaspoon paprika
1 teaspoon Worcestershire sauce
1½ teaspoons dry mustard
1 clove garlic
¼ cup canola oil

Combine all the ingredients in a blender and process until smooth. Store, tightly covered, in the refrigerator.

MAKES ABOUT 3½ CUPS

1 tablespoon contains approximately:
Calories / 21   Cholesterol / None
Fat / 1g   Sodium / 66mg

SALADS

When preparing salad greens it is important to wash and dry them thoroughly before storing them in bags or wrapping them in towels in the refrigerator. Wet salad greens dilute the dressing, and therefore you will be inclined to use more dressing on the salad. The thorough washing of the greens is one of the single most important steps in salad preparation. Nothing is worse than to be served a gritty salad; it can even be dangerous if you happen to bite down on a small rock in an innocent-looking salad.

When preparing spinach, it is necessary to fill the sink or a large tub or bowl with water and submerge the spinach completely, tearing off one leaf at a time in order to make certain that all the sandy dirt is removed. During the rainy season it is often necessary to wash lettuce and cabbage in the same manner because they tend to be caked with sand and dirt that cannot be removed any other way. With spinach it is also necessary to remove the stems and large veins that run down the backs of the leaves to take the bitter taste out of it. If you don't like spinach or spinach salad because of a slightly bitter aftertaste, you may find you have discovered a whole new vegetable when you eat it with the stems and veins removed.

Never put nuts or seeds on a salad or any other dish until you are ready to serve it. Otherwise the moisture will soften them and you won't get the delightful crunchiness that so enhances the texture of any dish.

SALAD GREENS GLOSSARY

ARUGULA: Sprigs of dark green leaves with a strong nutlike flavor. It combines well with mild-flavored lettuces or with equally intensely flavored greens, such as watercress.

BELGIAN ENDIVE: Also called French endive and witloof. Six- to eight-inch heads of crisp-tender yellow-white leaves with a green tinge. Delicately bitter flavor. Use whole or in bite-size pieces, thinly sliced (julienne cut). Mixes well with other greens. Expensive, but there is little waste.

BIBB LETTUCE: Also called butterhead, butter, limestone, or Boston lettuce. Soft, small, loosely formed heads with delicate leaves. Ranging in color from dark green to light yellow and buttery. They make ideal lettuce "bowls" for salads and mix well with other greens.

CABBAGE: The most widely used cabbage comes in compact heads of waxy, tightly wrapped leaves that range in color from almost white to green to red. Choose a cabbage with fresh, crisp-looking leaves that are firmly packed; the head should be heavy for its size. It can be cooked in a variety of ways or eaten raw.

CHICORY: Also called American or curly endive. Yellow-white stem with curly, fringed tendrils. Somewhat bitter taste. The outer leaves are darker and stronger flavored than the inner. A prickly texture to add to a tossed salad and an attractive garnish.

CHINESE CABBAGE: Also called Napa cabbage, Chinese celery cabbage, and sometimes bok choy, which is in the same family. Crinkly, thickly veined leaves that are cream-colored with green tips. The flavor is delicately mild and you can use it raw, sauté it, serve it baked or braised.

DANDELION GREENS: The wild variety is available in most places and is also especially grown for salads. The youngest leaves are the most tender. Slightly bitter.

ESCAROLE: Also called Batavian endive. The leaves are less curly and broader than endive and are a paler green; they should snap easily. Combine with other greens.

FENNEL: Also called anise. The stalks are similar to celery and grow from a bulbous root with lacy, fernlike leaves. The licoricelike flavor is more intense in the leaves, which are usually used as an herb. Substitute for celery in stuffings and casseroles. Slices of the bulb provide a uniquely different taste in salads.

FIDDLEHEAD: A fern often said to taste like asparagus, it is best in early spring when very young. Grows along stream banks.

FIELD LETTUCE: Also called lamb's lettuce, corn salad, and mache. Small, smooth green leaves in a loosely formed head. Tangy flavor good for tossed salads or as cooked greens.

ICEBERG LETTUCE: Also called crisphead lettuce. Large, compact heads with crisp leaves tightly packed. The outer leaves are a medium green and the inner leaves are a paler green. Slice, shred, or tear to add crunch to any salad. Longer shelf life than most lettuces.

ITALIAN PARSLEY: The sprigs have a flat, broad leaf rather than the tight, curly leaf of regular parsley, with a slightly milder flavor. A good garnish for Italian dishes.

LEAF LETTUCE: Loose, smooth leaves growing from a central stalk. Green or red-tipped curly leaves which make a good undergarnish for molded salads or fruits or vegetable arrangements.

MINT: Usually considered an herb, but important as a salad green in the Middle East, where it is an essential ingredient for the classic salad, tabbouleh. Also used as a garnish.

NASTURTIUM FLOWERS AND LEAVES: The leaves, stems, and flowers are all edible and interesting additions to salads. The leaves and stems have a pungent, peppery flavor. The flowers have a milder flavor and are a wonderful edible garniture.

PARSLEY: Dark green sprigs of tightly crimpled leaves with a strong, refreshing flavor. The leaves should be snipped or torn from the stems and the stems discarded. Usually thought of as a garnish, parsley is good in soups and for flavoring stocks. It is also good in salads of all types.

RADICCHIO: Small, cabbagelike head with red leaves. Flavor slightly bitter. Use as a garnish or mix with other greens to provide color and a different taste.

ROMAINE: Also called cos lettuce, and classically used for Caesar Salad. An elongated head of loose dark green leaves that are firm and crisp with a pungent flavor.

SORREL: Many edible varieties, both cultivated and wild. The arrow-shaped green leaves have a sour, almost bitter taste; the very young leaves are best. Best mixed with milder greens. Most frequently used in soups and sauces.

WATERCRESS: Dark green glossy leaves, dime-size, on crisp sprigs. The leaves and tender part of the stems are spicy and peppery. Good additions to tossed salads. Also often used as a garnish.

MARINATED CABBAGE SALAD

This salad will keep for at least two weeks and is best after two to three days.

> 2 *medium heads of cabbage (4 pounds), finely shredded (16 cups)*
> 2 *medium onions, thinly sliced and separated into rings (4 cups)*
> ¼ *cup sugar*
> ½ *cup unsweetened frozen apple juice concentrate*
> ¾ *cup cider vinegar*
> ¼ *cup canola oil*
> 1 *teaspoon dry mustard*
> 1 *teaspoon celery seed*
> 1 *teaspoon salt*

1. In a large bowl, alternate layers of shredded cabbage and onion rings. Sprinkle the sugar over the top and set aside.

2. In a saucepan over medium-high heat, combine all remaining ingredients and bring to a boil. Immediately pour the hot liquid over the cabbage mixture. Cover and refrigerate.

MAKES TWENTY-FOUR ½-CUP SERVINGS

Each serving contains approximately:
Calories / 68   Cholesterol / None
Fat / 3g   Sodium / 112mg

HEALTHY CABBAGE SALAD

This salad is best if made the day before you plan to serve it.

One 8-ounce package instant Chuka Soba noodles
1 head green cabbage, thinly sliced (12 cups)
8 scallions, chopped (2 cups)

DRESSING

½ cup unsweetened frozen apple juice concentrate, thawed
½ cup rice wine vinegar
3 tablespoons dark sesame oil
½ teaspoon salt
1 teaspoon freshly ground black pepper

½ cup chopped raw almonds, toasted in a preheated 350°F
oven until golden brown, 8 to 10 minutes

1. Bring 6 cups of water to a boil in a large pot. Add the noodles and boil 2 minutes, then drain thoroughly. Combine the cooked noodles, cabbage, and scallions in a large bowl.

2. Combine all the dressing ingredients except the almonds and mix well. Pour the dressing over the salad and mix thoroughly. Refrigerate for several hours, stirring occasionally so all the ingredients are thoroughly marinated.

3. To serve, place 1½ cups of the salad mixture on a large plate and top with 1 tablespoon of the toasted almonds. (I like the almonds better this way since they don't get soggy in the dressing.)

MAKES EIGHT 1½-CUP SERVINGS

Each serving contains approximately:
Calories / 283   Cholesterol / None
Fat / 11g   Sodium / 196mg

SUMMER CORN AND PEANUT PASTA SALAD

In the summer of 1992 I did a column on summer corn for *Cooking Light* magazine. This salad was one of the fresh corn recipes I have enjoyed using most. It is so colorful, tasty, and very easy to make. I called for farfalle pasta because the little bow-ties make such an attractive presentation but you can substitute any other small pasta such as elbows, rotini, or rotelle if you wish.

DRESSING

¼ *cup fresh lemon juice*
⅛ *teaspoon salt*
⅛ *teaspoon cayenne pepper*
3 *tablespoons unsweetened frozen apple juice concentrate, thawed*
2 *tablespoons rice wine vinegar*
1 *tablespoon dark sesame oil*

SALAD

6 *ounces farfalle, cooked according to package instructions (2 cups)*
2 *cups fresh corn kernels, steamed 3 minutes over rapidly boiling water*
1 *cup diced red bell pepper*
1 *cup diced green bell pepper*
¼ *cup chopped dry roasted peanuts for garnish*

1. To make the dressing, combine the lemon juice and salt in a small bowl. Stir until the salt is completely dissolved. Add the remaining ingredients and stir until well mixed (makes ½ cup dressing).

2. Combine the pasta with the dressing and the remaining salad ingredients, except the peanuts, in a large bowl and mix well.

Cover tightly with plastic wrap and refrigerate for several hours or overnight before serving. Stir occasionally to evenly distribute the dressing.

3. To serve, spoon 1 cup salad onto each of six chilled plates. Top each serving with 1 tablespoon peanuts.

MAKES SIX 1-CUP SERVINGS

Each serving contains approximately:
Calories / 229   Cholesterol / None
Fat / 6g   Sodium / 106mg

ENSALADA DE SEVILLA

This is the salad that was served by the Spanish Olive Oil Commission at a dinner they hosted in Madrid. It is a refreshing first course that pairs well with many entrées.

2 large or 3 medium oranges, peeled, sliced into rounds, and seeds removed
1 small onion, thinly sliced and separated into rings
2 tablespoons extra virgin olive oil
3 to 4 radishes, depending on size, thinly sliced for garnish

1. In a small bowl, combine half the orange slices and half the onion slices with 1 tablespoon of the oil. Repeat with the remaining orange and onion slices and oil. Allow to marinate, tightly covered, in the refrigerator for at least 2 hours. Marinating for many hours, or even overnight, will not harm the salad.

2. To serve, divide the salad onto four plates and spoon the juice and oil remaining in the bottom of the bowl evenly over each salad. Garnish with radish slices.

MAKES FOUR ¾-CUP SERVINGS

Each serving contains approximately:
Calories / 120   Cholesterol / None
Fat / 7g   Sodium / 4mg

SWEET AND LIGHT MACARONI SALAD

SALAD

3 pounds spiral macaroni, cooked according to package
 instructions
2 large carrots, shredded (2 cups)
1 large red onion, chopped (1½ cups)
1 large green bell pepper, seeded and chopped (1½ cups)
1 large cucumber, seeded and diced (1½ cups)

DRESSING

1 cup white vinegar
1½ cups sugar
⅓ cup mayonnaise
2 cups fat-free mayonnaise
⅔ cup skim milk
½ teaspoon salt

Combine all the salad ingredients in a very large bowl. In a medium-size bowl combine the dressing ingredients and add to the
salad. Mix well and refrigerate, tightly covered, for 12 hours or
overnight, before serving.

MAKES THIRTY 1-CUP SERVINGS

Each serving contains approximately:
Calories / 280   Cholesterol / 2mg
Fat / 3g   Sodium / 156mg

TUSCAN BEAN SALAD

This is a recipe I learned about at Lorenza di Medici's cooking school in Tuscany. I like it so much that I included it as part of a picnic dinner menu in my book *Jeanne Jones Entertains*. If you are making it for a picnic, don't add the tuna until you arrive and are ready to serve it.

1 cup dry white beans
2 tablespoons extra virgin olive oil
½ medium onion
3 tablespoons fresh lemon juice
½ teaspoon salt
½ teaspoon freshly ground black pepper
One 6½-ounce can water-packed tuna, drained and flaked
¼ cup chopped fresh basil leaves

1. Soak the beans overnight in cold water and drain. Put the beans in a large pot and cover with water. Cook, covered, over low heat for 1½ hours. Drain well and mix with the olive oil, then set aside.

2. Slice the onion vertically in paper-thin slices and soak in cold water for ½ hour, then drain thoroughly.

3. Combine the lemon juice, salt, and pepper and stir until the salt is dissolved. Add to the tuna and mix well.

4. Combine the beans, onion, tuna, and basil and mix well. Serve at room temperature.

MAKES FOUR 1¼-CUP SERVINGS

Each serving contains approximately:
Calories / 220   Cholesterol / 29mg
Fat / 8g   Sodium / 680mg

THAI CHICKEN SALAD

This is a salad I designed for the University of California, San Diego, Faculty Club. I am delighted to tell you that it is the biggest selling item on their menu.

THAI PEANUT DRESSING

⅓ *cup rice wine vinegar*
⅓ *cup smooth, unhomogenized peanut butter*
⅔ *cup water*
2 *tablespoons reduced-sodium soy sauce*
4 *cloves garlic*
2 *teaspoons sugar*
1 *teaspoon crushed red pepper flakes*

SALAD

2 *heads Boston (Bibb) lettuce*
2 *teaspoons dark sesame oil*
1 *large carrot, cut into thin strips*
1 *large green bell pepper, seeded and cut into thin strips*
½ *cup mung bean sprouts*
½ *cup chopped scallions*
½ *cup raisins*
5 *ounces cooked boneless, skinless chicken breast, cut into thin strips*
½ *cup cilantro leaves for garnish*

1. Combine all the dressing ingredients in a blender and process until smooth and set aside.

2. Remove the outside leaves of the lettuce and reserve for garnishing the plates. Shred the remaining lettuce and set aside (you should have 4 cups).

3. Heat the sesame oil in a medium-size skillet and cook the carrots and bell pepper strips over high heat until crisp-tender, 4 to 5 minutes, then set aside.

4. Arrange the reserved lettuce leaves on four plates. Top each with 1 cup shredded lettuce. Sprinkle 2 tablespoons each of the mung bean sprouts, scallions, and raisins over each salad and arrange 1¼ ounces chicken on top. Dress each salad with ¼ cup dressing, and divide the carrot and bell pepper evenly among each serving. Garnish with cilantro leaves.

MAKES 4 SERVINGS

Each serving contains approximately:
Calories / 310   Cholesterol / 30mg
Fat / 12g   Sodium / 197mg

VEGETABLES AND
VEGETARIAN ENTRÉES

In this section I have given you recipes for everything from small side dishes to hearty entrées. When planning your menus, don't decide which specific vegetables you are going to serve for each meal before going to the market. Then when you're shopping, select the freshest and most attractive vegetables available. The good news is that the freshest, best-looking, and most nutritious fruits and vegetables are the ones in season and therefore they are also the least expensive.

According to the American Cancer Society the new super-stars are the cruciferous vegetables, named for their cross-shaped flowers. They may actually help to prevent cancer and include broccoli, brussels sprouts, cabbage, cauliflower, and kohlrabi. Many of these vegetables have had star billing in the nutrition world for a long time. Vegetable stars of longer standing that still rate top billing in the medical world include spinach, carrots, garlic, onions, and potatoes. Of these ten top stars of the vegetable world, the only one that is not a relatively common everyday vegetable is kohlrabi. The kohlrabi looks like a large turnip but is actually a member of the cabbage family. It can be used in recipes to replace either turnips or potatoes and adds a strong but pleasant turniplike flavor.

Other tips for using some of the star-billed vegetables include the following:

- Treat broccoli as two separate vegetables, that is, use the stems and flowerettes separately. People often cut off the top part or flowerette cluster of the broccoli and throw the stems away. Instead, thinly slice them and steam them. Season them as you like and serve them as your vegetable.
- Remember to remove the stems and veins from spinach leaves and to scrape carrots in order to get rid of the bitterness in these two vegetables.
- Always keep onions in the refrigerator. When onions are cold, they do not release as much of the tear-producing gases for which they are so famous. Slicing them with a sharp as opposed to a dull knife also seems to help.
- When shredding potatoes to make hash browns or latkes, always soak them in cold water to wash away some of the potato starch. This gets rid of the gummy, chewy texture.

Steaming vegetables is the best method for cooking them because they retain more of their nutrients as well as their texture and color. All you need is a collapsible steamer basket and a pan with a tight-fitting lid. Add water to the pan to just below the basket level. Bring to a rapid boil, put the vegetables in the basket, and cover the pan. Set the timer, using the following steaming chart as a guide. This will give you al dente, or crisp-tender, vegetables every time. Remember, the minute you can smell a vegetable cooking, you are overcooking it. Overcooking vegetables destroys their texture and color as well as many valuable vitamins and minerals—and it smells up your house! Just as soon as the vegetables have cooked the prescribed time, remove the steamer basket from the pan and place it under cold running water. This stops the cooking process and preserves the color and texture.

This is the way good restaurants cook their vegetables; they then reheat them to serving temperature as orders come into the kitchen or refrigerate them to serve cold.

STEAMING TIME FOR FRESH VEGETABLES

Vegetable	Time (Minutes)	Vegetable	Time (Minutes)
Artichokes	30	Onions:	
Asparagus	5	green tops	3
Beets, quartered	15	whole	5
Broccoli:		Parsley	1–2
branches	5	Pea pods	3
flowerettes	3–5	Peas	3–5
Brussels sprouts	5	Peppers:	
Cabbage, quartered	5	bell	2
Carrots, ½-inch slices	5	chili	2–3
Cauliflower:		Potatoes:	
flowerettes	3	sweet, sliced	15
whole	5	white, sliced	10
Celery ribs	10	Pumpkin, cut up	5
Celery root	3–4	Rhubarb	5
Chard	1–2	Romaine lettuce	1–2
Chives	2–3	Rutabagas	8
Cilantro	1–2	Shallots	2
Corn kernels	3	Spinach	2
Corn on the cob	3	Squash:	
Cucumber, sliced	2–3	acorn, cut up	5
Eggplant, cut up	5	banana	5
Garlic	5	chayote	3
Kohlrabi	8–10	Hubbard, cut up	5
Leeks	5	summer	3
Lettuce	1–2	zucchini	3
Mushrooms	2	Tomatoes	3
Okra	5	Turnips, quartered	8
		Watercress	1–2

Vegetables can be easily reheated in a pan with a little water, defatted stock, juice, or wine instead of butter, margarine, or oil, and seasoned to taste. Be careful when reheating vegetables not to overcook them. Cold steamed vegetables make wonderful hors d'oeuvres and have a brighter color than raw vegetables when used in salads.

Other "light" approaches to cooking vegetables include stir-frying them without oil in the same way you would reheat steamed vegetables. Stir-fry them in either a wok or a skillet in water, defatted stock, juice, or wine. You can also blanch or parboil vegetables by plunging them into rapidly boiling water to cook them rather than cooking them above boiling water as in steaming. This method is generally used when you wish to only partially cook a vegetable before reheating or cooking it on a grill.

Using a microwave oven is still another cooking method. Follow the directions for your own oven for the timing. You can also bake vegetables, or broil or barbecue them. Let your imagination be your guide and learn to enjoy the full range of seasonal fresh vegetables. There really is no such thing as a vegetable that is not good for you.

GREEN RICE

1 tablespoon canola oil
1 medium onion, finely chopped (1½ cups)
2 pounds fresh spinach, well washed, large stems and veins
   removed, and chopped, or two 10-ounce packages frozen
   chopped spinach, thawed
3 cups cooked brown rice (instant is fastest)
¼ cup whole-wheat flour
8 ounces reduced-fat sharp Cheddar cheese, grated (2 cups)
2½ cups skim milk
¾ teaspoon salt
¼ teaspoon freshly ground black pepper

1. Preheat the oven to 350°F. Heat the oil in a skillet over low heat. Add the onion and cook, covered, until soft, about 10 minutes.

2. While the onion is cooking, steam the spinach for 1 minute (if using frozen steaming is not necessary). Squeeze the liquid from the spinach and set aside.

3. Combine the rice and the flour in a large bowl and mix well. Add the cooked onions, cheese, and spinach and again mix well. (Recipe may be made to this point and refrigerated to finish later in the day or even the next day.)

4. Combine the milk, salt, and pepper and add to the rice mixture. Mix well and spoon into a 2-quart ovenproof casserole. Bake until the liquid is absorbed, about 1¼ hours.

MAKES TWELVE ½-CUP SERVINGS

Each serving contains approximately:
Calories / 163   Cholesterol / 17mg
Fat / 6g   Sodium / 263mg

WILD RICE DRESSING

1 cup wild rice
2 cups defatted chicken stock
1½ teaspoons reduced-sodium soy sauce
1 tablespoon finely chopped fresh thyme
1 medium onion, finely chopped (1½ cups)
1 celery rib, without leaves, finely chopped (½ cup)

1. Combine the rice, 1¾ cups stock, soy sauce, and thyme in a medium-size saucepan. Bring to a boil, reduce the heat to low, cover, and simmer until all the liquid is absorbed and the rice is fluffy, 30 to 35 minutes. Remove from the heat and set aside.

2. Heat the remaining stock over medium heat in a skillet and add the chopped onion and celery. Sauté until the onion is clear and tender. Combine with the cooked rice, mixing well.

MAKES EIGHT ½-CUP SERVINGS

Each serving contains approximately:
Calories / 90   Cholesterol / None
Fat / Negligible   Sodium / 48mg

CAJUN RICE

1 cup tomato sauce
½ cup finely chopped celery
½ cup finely chopped green bell pepper
¼ cup finely chopped onion
½ teaspoon Tabasco sauce
½ teaspoon Cajun spices or Cajun Spice Mix (see page 100)
½ teaspoon oregano, crushed
2 cups cooked brown rice

1. Combine all the ingredients, except the rice, in a medium-size saucepan over low heat and cook until the vegetables are tender, about 30 minutes.

2. Add the rice and continue to cook until all the liquid is absorbed into the rice, about 20 to 30 minutes.

MAKES THREE 1-CUP SERVINGS

Each serving contains approximately:
Calories / 250   Cholesterol / None
Fat / 1g   Sodium / 625mg

OAT GROAT PILAF

Oat groats are hulled crushed oats. They are available in health food stores and in the health food sections of many larger markets.

> 1½ teaspoons corn oil
> 1 cup oat groats
> ½ medium onion, thinly sliced (1 cup)
> 1 tablespoon reduced-sodium soy sauce
> 1½ teaspoons fresh thyme, finely chopped, or ½ teaspoon dried, crushed
> 1¼ cups defatted chicken stock

1. Heat the oil in a heavy skillet over medium heat. Add the oat groats and onion and cook, stirring frequently, until brown.

2. Add the soy sauce and thyme to the stock in a small saucepan and bring to a boil.

3. Place the groat mixture in a 2-quart baking pan and add the hot stock. Stir to combine, then cover tightly. Place in a preheated 400°F oven for 1 hour. Remove and stir. Replace the cover and let stand for 10 minutes before serving.

4. To reheat, add 2 to 3 tablespoons of stock to the cold oat groat mixture and mix thoroughly. Cover and heat slowly in a preheated 300°F oven for about 25 minutes.

MAKES FOUR ½-CUP SERVINGS

Each serving contains approximately:
Calories / 200   Cholesterol / None
Fat / 5g   Sodium / 125mg

MAKE-AHEAD MASHED POTATOES

5 pounds Russet potatoes, peeled and quartered
6 ounces Neufchâtel cheese
1 cup light sour cream
2 teaspoons onion powder
1 teaspoon salt
½ teaspoon freshly ground black pepper
2 large egg whites
1 tablespoon corn-oil margarine

1. Place the potatoes in a 5- to 6-quart pot and add enough cold water to cover by one inch. Bring to a boil over high heat and boil until the potatoes are easily pierced with a fork. Drain well and mash with a potato masher until there are no lumps.

2. Add all the other ingredients, except the margarine, and blend well. Place in a 9-by-13-inch casserole that has been sprayed with nonstick vegetable spray, and dot with the margarine. If preparing ahead, allow to cool, cover, and refrigerate for several days if desired.

3. To serve, bake in a preheated 350°F oven for 40 minutes, or until hot.

MAKES TWELVE 1-CUP SERVINGS

Each serving contains approximately:
Calories / 201   Cholesterol / 19mg
Fat / 7g   Sodium / 291mg

POTATOES IN THE OVEN

2½ tablespoons corn-oil margarine
1 clove garlic, minced
¼ cup plus 1½ teaspoons unbleached all-purpose flour
1 cup defatted chicken stock
¾ cup skim milk
½ teaspoon salt (omit if using salted stock)
Dash of freshly ground black pepper
¼ cup finely chopped cooked chicken
6 medium baking potatoes, peeled and diced (8 cups)
¼ cup finely chopped onion
¼ teaspoon ground white or black pepper
6 ounces reduced-fat Cheddar cheese, shredded (1½ cups)
⅔ cup light sour cream
½ cup soft whole-wheat bread crumbs

1. Preheat the oven to 350°F. Melt 1½ tablespoons of the margarine in a skillet over medium heat, then add the garlic and cook, stirring, just until it sizzles. Add the flour and stir for 1 minute. Do not brown. Add the stock and milk slowly and, using a wire whisk, stir the mixture until it comes to a boil. Add the salt, pepper, and chicken, and continue to cook for 1 minute more.

2. Spray a large baking dish with nonstick vegetable coating. Mix together the stock mixture, potatoes, onion, pepper, cheese, and sour cream. Pour into the baking dish.

3. Melt the remaining 1 tablespoon of margarine in a skillet. Mix with the bread crumbs and sprinkle over the potato mixture. Cover and bake until the potatoes are tender and the casserole is hot and bubbly, about 1 hour.

MAKES EIGHT 1-CUP SERVINGS

Each serving contains approximately:
Calories / 287   Cholesterol / 30mg
Fat / 12g   Sodium / 311mg

NEW BAKED CORN

One 17-ounce can cream-style corn
½ cup liquid egg substitute
1 tablespoon corn-oil margarine, melted
2 tablespoons finely chopped green bell pepper
2 tablespoons unbleached all-purpose flour
¼ cup skim milk
½ teaspoon salt

1. Preheat the oven to 350°F. Combine all the ingredients in a large bowl and mix thoroughly. Pour into an ovenproof dish or pan which can be placed inside another. Pour hot water into the outer dish or pan.

2. Bake until a knife inserted in the center comes out clean, about 1 hour.

MAKES TEN ¼-CUP SERVINGS

Each serving contains approximately:
Calories / 64   Cholesterol / Negligible
Fat / 2g   Sodium / 297mg

"LIGHT" CREAMED ONIONS

6 medium brown or Spanish onions, sliced crosswise into ⅜-inch slices
1 cup water
2 tablespoons corn-oil margarine
2 tablespoons unbleached all-purpose flour
¾ cup skim milk
½ teaspoon salt
¼ teaspoon ground white pepper
½ cup plain bread crumbs
1 tablespoon corn-oil margarine, melted

1. Combine the onions and water in a large saucepan and bring to a boil. Reduce heat to low and cook, covered, until the onions are tender, about 10 minutes. Drain, reserving ½ cup of the liquid.

2. Melt the margarine in a medium-size saucepan. Add the flour and cook until bubbly, stirring constantly.

3. Combine the milk with the liquid reserved from cooking the onions and gradually add to the flour mixture, stirring constantly. Cook until the mixture is thickened and comes to a boil, stirring constantly. Add the salt and pepper and mix well.

4. Remove from the heat. Place the onions in a casserole and pour the sauce over them. Combine the bread crumbs and the melted margarine and mix well. Sprinkle over the casserole. Bake in a preheated 350°F oven until the top is lightly browned and the sauce begins to bubble, about 25 minutes.

MAKES EIGHT ¾-CUP SERVINGS

Each serving contains approximately:
Calories / 160   Cholesterol / 1mg
Fat / 5g   Sodium / 260mg

SWEET ONION CASSEROLE

1 pound Vidalia or other sweet onions, thinly sliced and
  separated into rings
1 cup buttermilk
1 tablespoon cornstarch
2 large egg whites
½ teaspoon salt
½ teaspoon freshly ground black pepper
2 ounces shredded reduced-fat sharp Cheddar cheese
Paprika for garnish

1. Preheat the oven to 350°F. In medium-size saucepan, combine the onions with water to cover. Bring to a boil and boil 1 minute. Drain well. Transfer to an 8-inch-square baking dish sprayed with nonstick vegetable coating.

2. In a bowl combine the buttermilk and cornstarch and stir until the cornstarch is completely dissolved. Mix in the egg whites, salt, and pepper, and pour over the onions. Sprinkle evenly with the cheese, then the paprika. Bake until the cheese is melted and the casserole is set, about 25 minutes.

MAKES SIX ⅓-CUP SERVINGS

Each serving contains approximately:
Calories / 83   Cholesterol / 9mg
Fat / 3g   Sodium / 292mg

GOLD COIN CARROTS

One 10-ounce package frozen peas
2 pounds carrots, peeled and sliced
1 medium red onion, thinly sliced and separated into rings
1 small green bell pepper, seeded and sliced
One 8-ounce can tomato sauce
1 tablespoon canola oil
1 cup frozen unsweetened apple juice concentrate, thawed
1 tablespoon pure crystalline fructose or 1½ tablespoons sugar
¾ cup cider vinegar
1 teaspoon Worcestershire sauce
½ teaspoon salt
¼ teaspoon freshly ground black pepper

1. Place the carrots in a medium-size saucepan with a small amount of water. Cover and cook over medium heat until crisp-tender, about 5 minutes; do not overcook. Rinse under cold water to stop the cooking, drain, and cool.

2. In a medium-size bowl, alternate layers of cooked carrots, peas, onion rings, and bell pepper slices.

3. In another medium-size bowl, mix the remaining ingredients until smooth. Pour over the vegetables, cover, and refrigerate overnight. May be held refrigerated for up to two weeks.

MAKES EIGHT ¾-CUP SERVINGS

Each serving contains approximately:
Calories / 185   Cholesterol / None
Fat / 2g   Sodium / 450mg

LIVELY LIMAS

1 pound dried lima beans, rinsed and picked over
1 teaspoon cornstarch
1 cup canned evaporated skimmed milk
⅓ cup firmly packed brown sugar
¼ cup dark molasses
2 tablespoons prepared mustard
½ teaspoon salt

1. Soak the lima beans overnight in 8 cups of water. Drain and place in a large saucepan with 8 more cups of water. Cook, covered, over low heat until tender, about 1 hour. Drain well.

2. In a large bowl, dissolve the cornstarch in the milk. Stir in the brown sugar, molasses, mustard, and salt until well combined.

3. Gently fold the drained limas into the molasses mixture, then pour into a casserole that has been sprayed with nonstick vegetable coating. Bake for 45 minutes in a preheated 350°F oven.

MAKES EIGHT ¾-CUP SERVINGS

Each serving contains approximately:
Calories / 152   Cholesterol / 1mg
Fat / 1g   Sodium / 238mg

HOMEMADE BROCCOLI OR CAULIFLOWER CASSEROLE

1½ pounds broccoli or cauliflower, cut into flowerettes (6 cups)
1 tablespoon corn-oil margarine
1 clove garlic, minced
3 tablespoons unbleached all-purpose flour
¾ cup defatted chicken stock
½ cup skim milk
¼ teaspoon salt (omit if using salted stock)
Dash of freshly ground black pepper
2 ounces fresh mushrooms, steamed 2 minutes and finely chopped (¼ cup)
⅓ cup reduced-calorie mayonnaise
1 tablespoon fresh lemon juice
2 ounces reduced-fat sharp Cheddar cheese, grated (½ cup)
¼ cup unblanched almonds, sliced and toasted in a 350°F oven until golden brown, 8 to 10 minutes

1.   Steam the broccoli or cauliflower, or a combination of each, 3 to 5 minutes, until crisp-tender. Immediately rinse under cold water, drain well, and place in a 2-quart casserole dish.

2.   Melt the margarine in a saucepan over medium heat, then add the garlic and cook, stirring, just until it sizzles. Add the flour and stir for 1 minute; do not brown. Add the chicken stock and

milk slowly and cook, stirring constantly with a whisk, until the mixture comes to a boil. Add the salt, pepper, and mushrooms and continue to cook for 1 minute more.

3. Remove the mixture from the heat and stir in the mayonnaise, lemon juice, and grated cheese. Pour over the vegetables and sprinkle with the toasted almonds. Bake in a preheated 350°F oven until the sauce is hot and bubbly, about 30 minutes.

MAKES FOUR 1-CUP SERVINGS

Each serving contains approximately:
Calories / 258   Cholesterol / 19mg
Fat / 18g   Sodium / 424mg

BROCCOLI-MUSHROOM MOLD

3¾ pounds broccoli, ends trimmed and stalks peeled
2 teaspoons corn-oil margarine
1 teaspoon canola oil
½ pound mushrooms, finely chopped and dried with paper towels
¼ cup minced onion
⅓ cup minced shallots
1¼ cups liquid egg substitute
½ cup fine plain bread crumbs
½ cup low-fat milk
⅛ teaspoon freshly grated nutmeg
½ teaspoon salt
⅛ teaspoon freshly ground black pepper

1. Cut the broccoli flowerettes from the stalks close to their base. Steam the flowerettes until bright green, 3 minutes. Rinse under cold water until cold and set aside.

2. Chop the broccoli stalks and steam until tender, 10 minutes. Drain and puree in a food processor with a metal blade or in a blender. Pour into a mixing bowl and set aside.

3. In a 10-inch skillet over medium heat, combine 1 teaspoon of the margarine and the oil. Cook the mushrooms, onion, and shallots, stirring, until the moisture evaporates. Add the mushroom mixture to the broccoli puree, then mix in the egg substitute, bread crumbs, milk, nutmeg, salt, and pepper.

4. Pour the mixture into 1½-quart ring mold sprayed with nonstick vegetable coating. Set the mold in a pan filled with enough hot water to reach halfway up the sides of the mold. Bake in a preheated 325°F oven until set, 40 to 45 minutes. Cool 5 minutes before unmolding onto a warmed serving platter.

5. In a large skillet over medium heat, melt the remaining margarine. Toss the reserved flowerettes in the pan for a few minutes until hot. Arrange the flowerettes in the center and around the outer edge of the mold.

MAKES TWELVE 1-CUP SERVINGS

Each serving contains approximately:
Calories / 104   Cholesterol / 1mg
Fat / 3g   Sodium / 238mg

PASTA WITH MUSHROOMS

2 tablespoons extra virgin olive oil
1 clove garlic, pressed or minced
½ pound fresh mushrooms, sliced (2 cups)
4 ounces freshly grated Parmesan cheese (1 cup)
1 pound fettuccine, cooked according to package instructions
Fresh basil leaves, for garnish

1. Heat 1 tablespoon of the oil in a large skillet over medium-low heat. Cook the garlic, stirring, just until it starts to sizzle. Add the mushrooms, cover, and cook until soft, stirring occasionally.

2. Toss the remaining oil and ½ cup of the cheese with the hot cooked pasta. Place 2 cups of the pasta on each of four plates and sprinkle 2 tablespoons of cheese over the top of each serving. Divide the mushroom-and-garlic mixture evenly over each serving and garnish with fresh basil. Serve with a lightly dressed green salad with fresh tomato slices and a crusty Italian bread.

MAKES FOUR 2-CUP SERVINGS

Each serving contains approximately:
Calories / 470   Cholesterol / 15mg
Fat / 14g   Sodium / 348mg

"MODERN" MUSHROOM SOUFFLÉ

8 slices whole-wheat bread, crusts removed
1½ cups skim milk
2 tablespoons corn-oil margarine
¾ cup chopped onion
1½ pounds fresh mushrooms, chopped (8 cups)
¾ teaspoon salt
2 tablespoons minced fresh parsley
1 large egg yolk, lightly beaten
3 large egg whites, beaten until soft peaks form
2 tablespoons plain bread crumbs

1. Preheat the oven to 350°F. Soak the bread in the milk for 15 minutes, then mash thoroughly and set aside.

2. In a large skillet over medium heat, melt the margarine. Add the onion and cook for 5 minutes. Add the mushrooms and cook until soft, about 5 to 7 minutes more.

3. In a large mixing bowl, combine the mashed bread and mushroom mixture. Add the salt, parsley, and egg yolk and mix well. Fold in the egg whites until no streaks of white show and spoon into a 3-quart casserole or soufflé dish that has been sprayed with nonstick vegetable coating. Sprinkle the top with the bread crumbs and bake until a knife inserted in the center comes out clean, about 1 hour. Serve immediately. (Leftovers are wonderful for breakfast.)

MAKES SIX 1-CUP SERVINGS

Each serving contains approximately:
Calories / 190   Cholesterol / 38mg
Fat / 6g   Sodium / 598mg

"MAGIC" ZUCCHINI CASSEROLE

¾ *pound zucchini, thinly sliced (3 cups)*
1 *medium onion, diced (1½ cups)*
2 *tablespoons canola oil*
½ *cup plus 1 tablespoon freshly grated Parmesan cheese*
1 *cup light biscuit mix*
1 *cup liquid egg substitute or 2 large eggs and 3 egg whites,*
   lightly beaten
1 *clove garlic, minced*

1. Spray a 7-by-11-inch or 9-inch-square baking dish with nonstick vegetable coating. Combine all the ingredients except 1 tablespoon of the Parmesan cheese and pour into the dish.

2. Sprinkle with the remaining cheese and bake in a preheated 350°F oven until the top is golden brown, 30 to 40 minutes.

MAKES 6 SERVINGS

Each serving contains approximately:
Calories / 199   Cholesterol / 7mg
Fat / 11g   Sodium / 342mg

SPINACH WITH RAISINS

½ *cup raisins*
2 *tablespoons pine nuts*
2 *pounds fresh spinach, well washed, or two 10-ounce*
   packages frozen, thawed
1 *tablespoon extra virgin olive oil*
¼ *teaspoon salt*

1. Soak the raisins in warm water to cover for 30 minutes, then drain and pat dry. While the raisins are soaking, preheat the oven to 350°F. Toast the pine nuts on an ungreased baking sheet until golden brown, about 5 minutes. Watch carefully, as they burn easily. Set aside.

2. Remove the stems and large veins from the fresh spinach. Place the spinach in a steamer basket over rapidly boiling water and steam for 1½ minutes. Immediately rinse the spinach under cold running water to intensify the color and drain thoroughly. (If you are using thawed frozen spinach, it is not necessary to steam it. Simply go on to the next step.)

3. Heat the olive oil and salt in a large saucepan over medium heat. Add the spinach and raisins and cook, stirring, until the spinach is thoroughly heated. Top each serving with 1½ teaspoons of toasted pine nuts.

MAKES FOUR ½-CUP SERVINGS

Each serving contains approximately:
Calories / 132   Cholesterol / None
Fat / 5g   Sodium / 247mg

SPINACH FRITTATA

1 pound spinach, stems and large veins removed, washed, and chopped
1 tablespoon extra virgin olive oil
1 tablespoon minced onion
¾ cup liquid egg substitute
¼ cup freshly grated Parmesan cheese
½ teaspoon dried oregano, crushed
⅛ teaspoon freshly ground black pepper

1. Steam the spinach over rapidly boiling water for 2 minutes. Immediately rinse under cold running water, drain well, and then squeeze out any remaining moisture. You should have about 1 cup of chopped spinach. Set aside.

2. Heat the oil in an ovenproof 8-inch skillet or omelet pan over low heat. Add the onion and cook, stirring, until clear and tender, about 8 to 10 minutes.

3. In a small bowl, combine the egg substitute with half the cheese, oregano, pepper, and spinach and mix well.

4. Pour the egg mixture into the skillet and cook over very low heat until the edges are lightly browned. Sprinkle the remaining cheese over the top and place under a preheated broiler until the cheese is lightly browned. To serve, cut into wedges.

MAKES 4 SERVINGS

Each serving contains approximately:
Calories / 106   Cholesterol / 4mg
Fat / 6g   Sodium / 212mg

CHILIES RELLENOS

2 tablespoons corn-oil margarine
One 7-ounce can whole green chilies, rinsed, drained, and cut
  into 1-inch-wide strips
8 ounces reduced-fat Monterey Jack cheese, shredded (2 cups)
4 ounces reduced-fat Cheddar cheese, shredded (1 cup)
6 large egg whites, lightly beaten
1 tablespoon corn oil
1 tablespoon instant nonfat dry milk
½ teaspoon salt
1 cup light biscuit mix
2 cups skim milk

1. Preheat the oven to 350°F. Melt the margarine in a 9-by-13-inch baking dish and tilt to cover the bottom of the dish. Lay the chilies evenly over the margarine.

2. Combine the shredded cheeses and spread evenly over the chilies. Combine the egg whites, oil, dry milk, salt, biscuit mix, and milk, and mix well, using a wire whisk. Pour over the cheeses. Bake until a light golden brown, 40 to 45 minutes.

MAKES 9 SERVINGS

Each serving contains approximately:
Calories / 247   Cholesterol / 33mg
   Fat / 15g   Sodium / 778mg

NOT-SO-RICH CHEESE AND ONION PIE

1 tablespoon water
1 large onion, chopped (2 cups)
3 large egg whites
1 tablespoon instant nonfat dry milk
1 tablespoon canola oil
1 cup canned evaporated skimmed milk
½ teaspoon salt
⅛ teaspoon ground white pepper
⅛ teaspoon freshly grated nutmeg
8 ounces reduced-fat Swiss cheese, grated (2 cups)
Prepared 9-inch pie crust (optional)

1. Combine the water and onion in a microwave-safe bowl. Cover and cook 3 minutes on high in microwave oven. Leave covered and let stand 5 minutes. (Or cook in a covered skillet over low heat until the onion is tender, about 10 minutes, stirring frequently.) Drain off any liquid that has accumulated.

2. Combine the egg whites, dry milk, oil, evaporated milk, salt, pepper, and nutmeg. Stir in the cheese and onion. Carefully pour the mixture into a quiche pan or 9-inch pie plate, or into a prepared crust. Bake in a preheated 375°F oven until the center is set and the top is golden brown, about 30 to 35 minutes. Let stand 10 minutes before slicing.

MAKES 6 SERVINGS

Each serving contains approximately:
Calories / 200   Cholesterol / 30mg
Fat / 8g   Sodium / 360mg

LOW-CHOLESTEROL ARTICHOKE/CHEESE PIE

2 teaspoons corn-oil margarine
2 tablespoons tarragon or cider vinegar
1 small onion, finely chopped (1 cup)
1 clove garlic, minced
One 7¾-ounce can artichoke hearts, drained and chopped
1 cup liquid egg substitute, lightly beaten
¼ cup fine plain bread crumbs
¼ teaspoon dried basil, crushed
⅛ teaspoon dried oregano, crushed
¼ teaspoon salt
Freshly ground black pepper to taste
Dash of Tabasco sauce
2 tablespoons minced fresh parsley
8 ounces reduced-fat Swiss or Cheddar cheese, shredded
  (2 cups)

1. Preheat the oven to 325°F. Melt the margarine in a non-stick pan over medium heat, add the vinegar, onion, and garlic, and cook, stirring, until soft, then set aside.

2. Add the chopped artichoke hearts to the liquid egg substitute in a large bowl. Stir in the remaining ingredients, adding the onion mixture and the cheese last.

3. Spray a 9-inch pie or quiche pan with nonstick vegetable coating. Pour the mixture into the pan and bake until set, about 30 to 35 minutes. Serve hot.

MAKES 8 SERVINGS

Each serving contains approximately:
Calories / 120   Cholesterol / 15mg
Fat / 5g   Sodium / 217mg

MEXICAN QUICHE

1 cup liquid egg substitute
¼ cup unbleached all-purpose flour
½ teaspoon baking powder
1 tablespoon corn-oil margarine, melted
1 cup low-fat cottage cheese
6 ounces reduced-fat Monterey Jack cheese, shredded
   (1½ cups)
One 4-ounce can diced green chilies

1. Spray a 9-by-9-inch pan with nonstick vegetable coating. Combine the egg substitute, flour, and baking powder in a medium-size bowl, and blend well. Add the melted margarine, cottage chese, Jack cheese, and chilies, and mix just until blended.

2. Pour the mixture into the prepared pan and bake in a preheated 400°F for 15 minutes. Reduce the heat to 350°F and continue baking until the top is golden and the quiche is set, about an additional 30 to 35 minutes. Cut into small squares and serve hot as an appetizer or into larger squares for six brunch servings.

MAKES 6 SERVINGS

Each serving contains approximately:
Calories / 202   Cholesterol / 28mg
Fat / 11g   Sodium / 608mg

POTATO, SHIITAKE, AND BRIE GRATIN

6 good-size new red potatoes, scrubbed but not peeled and cut
   into ⅛-inch-thick slices
8 ounces shiitake mushrooms, stems removed and caps thinly
   sliced
6 ounces fairly firm Brie, rind removed and cut into small
   cubes

½ teaspoon salt
Freshly ground black pepper to taste
1 cup canned evaporated skimmed milk
2 teaspoons corn-oil margarine, melted
2 cloves garlic, minced
1 teaspoon dried thyme, crushed
2 tablespoons freshly grated Parmesan cheese
¼ cup fine dry plain bread crumbs

1. Place the potato slices in a large bowl of cold water and soak for 30 minutes, changing the water twice. Drain and pat dry.

2. Preheat the oven to 425°F. Spray a shallow gratin dish or glass baking dish about 10 inches across with nonstick spray, preferably butter-flavored.

3. Layer a third of the potato slices in the dish, then lay half the shiitakes and half the cheese evenly over them. Season with ¼ teaspoon salt and pepper to taste. Add another third of the potatoes and top with the remaining shiitakes and Brie. Season with the remaining salt and pepper to taste. Arrange the remaining potato slices on top. Combine the milk, margarine, garlic, and thyme and pour over the potatoes, pushing down so that all the liquid is absorbed. Cover the dish tightly with aluminum foil and bake 30 minutes.

4. Combine the Parmesan cheese and bread crumbs. Remove the foil and sprinkle the mixture over the potatoes. Place the dish on a rack in the bottom third of the oven and bake until the potatoes are very tender and the top and bottom are crusty and dark brown, 30 to 40 minutes longer.

MAKES 6 SERVINGS

Each serving contains approximately:
Calories / 285   Cholesterol / 31mg
Fat / 10g   Sodium / 520mg

LIGHT AUTUMN RAREBIT

1 tablespoon Dijon mustard
1 tablespoon Worcestershire sauce
1 tablespoon curry powder
1 teaspoon caraway seeds
½ teaspoon paprika
½ teaspoon salt
Pinch of cayenne pepper
1 cup ale
8 cups (2 pounds) grated reduced-fat Cheddar cheese

1. In the top of a double boiler, combine all the ingredients except the cheese. Mix well and heat over gently boiling water.

2. Reduce the heat to medium-low and gradually add the cheese, whisking constantly until all the cheese is melted and the mixture is hot.

MAKES NINE ½-CUP SERVINGS

Each serving contains approximately:
Calories / 260 Cholesterol / 85mg
Fat / 16g Sodium / 464mg

FISH AND SEAFOOD

Fish and shellfish are excellent sources of vitamins and minerals and supply many of the minerals, such as iodine, zinc, and selenium, that are scarce in most other food sources. Canned fish which includes the bones, such as salmon, sardines, and anchovies, is extremely high in calcium.

When buying a whole fresh fish, always look at the eyes. If the fish is really fresh, the eyes will be very clear. As it gets older, the eyes become cloudy-looking. The scales of a fresh fish will not be separated from the skin. Filleted fresh fish should look moist and never as though it is drying out. Also, fresh fish and seafood do not have the overly strong "fishy" smell many people dislike. If the odor of the fish is too strong, you can be sure the fish is not fresh.

Shellfish are often suspected of coming from contaminated water. Be aware of where the shellfish originates and the water conditions prevailing in that area.

The storage of fresh fish is equally important. Immediately unwrap fish you have purchased and wash it under cold running water. Dry it thoroughly and squeeze fresh lemon juice all over the surface. Store it in a nonaluminum container tightly covered in the refrigerator. If you must keep it for more than a day before serving, place the container on a pan over ice cubes in the refrigerator.

When fresh fish is not available, it is often necessary to buy frozen fish. When using frozen fish, always put it in the refrigerator to thaw so that it thaws slowly. If you force the thawing time, the texture of the fish will be mushy and very unappetizing. After frozen fish has thawed, handle it exactly the same way you would fresh fish. It should not be refrozen.

There are many wonderful canned fish and seafood products that you can keep in your cupboard and always have on hand. These include water-packed tuna, clams packed in clam juice, oysters, salmon, sardines, and anchovies.

When cooking fish the single most important thing to remember is not to overcook it. The minute it turns from translucent to opaque, it is done. Further cooking will only lessen the flavor and make the fish tough and dry. When poaching shellfish such as shrimp and scallops, it will literally take no more than a minute or two in a boiling stock or court bouillon.

FISH STOCK

There is nothing better than a good fish stock for poaching fish and seafood, or for making rich fish soup or stew. I also like to use fish stock to moisten the pan for sautéing or braising fish or seafood. When fish heads are not available, I often make a shellfish stock using shrimp, crab, or lobster shells.

3 quarts water
¼ cup vinegar
2 pounds fish heads, bones, and trimmings
2 onions, sliced
5 parsley sprigs
1 carrot, sliced
½ teaspoon dried marjoram, crushed
¼ teaspoon peppercorns
½ teaspoon salt
1 tablespoon fresh lemon juice

Bring all of the ingredients to a boil in a large saucepan, reduce the heat to low, and simmer for 40 minutes. Line a colander or strainer with damp cheesecloth and strain the fish stock through it. Cool to room temperature and refrigerate. Freeze any stock you are not going to use immediately in containers of a volume you most frequently use.

MAKES 8 CUPS

1 cup contains approximately:
Calories / Negligible   Cholesterol / Negligible
Fat / Negligible   Sodium / Varies

COURT BOUILLON

Anytime you are going to cook shrimp, crabs, or lobster, or poach any fish, prepare a court bouillon first. Of course you can use fish stock for poaching fish, but this court bouillon is much faster and easier to make and completely satisfactory. You just cannot compare seafood cooked in plain, salty water to the seafood cooked in court bouillon.

4 cups water
¼ cup white vinegar
½ lemon, sliced
1 celery rib, without leaves, sliced
1 carrot, scraped and sliced
½ onion, sliced
1 clove garlic
1 bay leaf
¼ teaspoon peppercorns
1½ teaspoons salt

Combine all the ingredients in a medium-size saucepan and bring to a boil. Reduce the heat to low and simmer for 45 minutes. This court bouillon may be made ahead and used many times. When doing this, strain before storing. After each use, store in the freezer.

MAKES 4 CUPS

1 cup contains approximately:
Calories / Negligible   Cholesterol / Negligible
Fat / Negligible   Sodium / Varies

SHRIMP AMANDINE

3 pounds medium shrimp, peeled and deveined
¼ cup extra virgin olive oil
½ cup fresh lemon juice
½ cup clam juice or defatted, unsalted chicken stock
2 cloves garlic, finely chopped
½ cup shallots
2 dashes Tabasco sauce
¼ teaspoon salt
¼ cup dry white wine or vermouth
½ cup chopped raw almonds, toasted in a 350°F oven until
  golden brown, 8 to 10 minutes

1. Marinate the shrimp in the olive oil, lemon juice, clam juice, and garlic, for about 2 hours in the refrigerator.

2. Remove the shrimp from the marinade and transfer the marinade to a large skillet. Bring it to a boil over medium heat, then cook the shallots and shrimp, stirring, until the shrimp are pink, about 4 minutes. Remove the shrimp and shallots and place on a warm platter.

3. Add the Tabasco, salt, and wine to the marinade in the skillet and let simmer 3 to 4 minutes. Pour over the shrimp and sprinkle the toasted almonds over the top. Serve over rice.

MAKES SIX 1½-CUP SERVINGS

Each serving contains approximately:
Calories / 379   Cholesterol / 340mg
Fat / 16g   Sodium / 491mg

SHRIMP CREOLE

3 pounds medium shrimp, peeled and deveined
1 medium onion, chopped (1½ cups)
1 clove garlic, minced
2 celery ribs, chopped
1 small green bell pepper, chopped (1 cup)
One 8-ounce can whole tomatoes
One half 6-ounce can tomato paste
1 bay leaf
3 sprigs fresh thyme
1 tablespoon finely chopped fresh parsley
½ teaspoon sugar
¼ teaspoon salt
¼ teaspoon freshly ground black pepper

1. Bring a large saucepan of water to a boil. Drop in the shrimp and let boil until they turn from translucent to opaque, about 2 minutes. Set aside.

2. Cook the onion and garlic, covered, over low heat in a large saucepan, until soft. Add a little water if necessary to prevent scorching. Add the celery and bell pepper, cover, and cook 5 more minutes.

3. Add the tomatoes, tomato paste, and seasonings, cover, and let simmer for 30 minutes.

4. Add the shrimp and mix thoroughly until heated through. Serve in a circle of cooked rice.

MAKES EIGHT 1½-CUP SERVINGS

Each serving contains approximately:
Calories / 188   Cholesterol / 255mg
Fat / 2g   Sodium / 409mg

LIGHT GARLIC SHRIMP AND OYSTERS WITH PASTA

*½ teaspoon each: ground white pepper, onion powder, cayenne
pepper, paprika, dried thyme, and freshly ground black
pepper*
1 tablespoon unsalted corn-oil margarine
3 tablespoons defatted chicken stock
3 scallions, chopped (½ cup)
3 ounces medium shrimp, peeled and deveined
3 cloves garlic, minced
One 8-ounce can oysters, chopped and liquid reserved
⅓ pound spaghetti, cooked according to package instructions

1. Combine the spices in a small bowl. Melt the margarine
in a skillet and add the stock, spice mixture, scallions, shrimp, and
garlic. Cook over medium-high heat until the shrimp turn pink,
vigorously shaking the pan in a back-and-forth motion, about 1
minute.

2. Add the oysters and their liquid. Cook until the oysters
are heated, continuing to shake the pan, about 1 minute. Add the
spaghetti, toss, and cook until the pasta is heated through, about
1 minute. Serve immediately.

MAKES FOUR 1-CUP SERVINGS

Each serving contains approximately:
Calories / 258   Cholesterol / 57mg
Fat / 5g   Sodium / 291mg

PASTA WITH SHRIMP AND WINE

1 tablespoon plus 2 teaspoons corn-oil margarine
1 teaspoon olive oil
½ large onion, chopped (1 cup)
½ cup dry white wine
1 cup defatted chicken stock, reduced to ½ cup over medium-high heat in a saucepan
1 teaspoon dried basil, crushed
½ teaspoon salt (omit if using salted stock)
⅛ teaspoon freshly ground black pepper
12 ounces raw shrimp, peeled, deveined and halved lengthwise
2 medium, ripe tomatoes, peeled, seeded, and chopped (1 cup)
10 ounces linguine, cooked according to package instructions
½ cup freshly grated Parmesan cheese
½ cup loosely packed fresh parsley, without stems

1. In a large saucepan, heat 2 teaspoons of the margarine with the olive oil. When the margarine melts, cook the onions over medium heat until transparent, stirring occasionally. Stir in the wine, stock, basil, salt, and pepper. Bring to a boil. Reduce the heat slightly and boil gently, uncovered, until reduced in volume by two thirds, about 12 minutes. (You should have about ¾ cup liquid.)

2. Reduce the heat to low and add the shrimp. Simmer, covered, for 3 to 5 minutes, just until the shrimp are tender. Remove from the heat and stir in the tomatoes.

3. Toss the hot cooked pasta with the remaining margarine in a large serving bowl. Add the shrimp mixture, the cheese, and parsley, and toss until the pasta is coated. Serve immediately.

MAKES 4 SERVINGS

Each serving contains approximately:
Calories / 480   Cholesterol / 137mg
Fat / 12g   Sodium / 685mg

SHRIMP AND WILD RICE

2 teaspoons corn-oil margarine
1 medium carrot, chopped (½ cup)
1 medium celery rib, chopped (½ cup)
3 medium scallions with tops, chopped (1 cup)
⅓ cup long-grain brown rice
⅓ cup wild rice
2 tablespoons dried parsley
2 tablespoons dried onion
½ teaspoon celery salt
½ teaspoon paprika
¼ teaspoon garlic powder
¼ teaspoon sugar
¼ teaspoon freshly ground black pepper
⅛ teaspoon turmeric
1⅔ cups defatted chicken stock or water
1 pound large shrimp, peeled and deveined

SAUCE

1½ cups skim milk
½ teaspoon salt
3 tablespoons uncooked Cream of Rice cereal
¼ cup sherry
Freshly ground black pepper to taste
Tabasco sauce to taste

1. Melt the margarine in a large saucepan over medium heat. Add the carrot, celery, and scallions and cook, stirring, 3 to 4 minutes. Add all the remaining ingredients, except the shrimp. Bring to a boil and then simmer over medium-low heat, covered, until the rice is tender and the liquid is absorbed, about 55 minutes.

2. While the rice mixture is simmering, cook the shrimp and prepare the sauce. Bring 4 cups of water to boil in a 2-quart saucepan. Add the shrimp, cover, and as soon as the water begins to boil again reduce the heat and simmer just until the shrimp are

pink and firm, 3 to 5 minutes. Rinse under cold water to stop the cooking, drain thoroughly, and set aside.

3. Bring the milk and salt to a boil in a small saucepan. Add the Cream of Rice and stir for 1 minute. Remove from the heat, cover, and allow to stand 5 minutes.

4. Pour the sauce mixture into a blender along with six shrimp. Blend until smooth. Pour back into the saucepan, and add the sherry, pepper, and Tabasco. Cook over low heat until heated through.

5. When the rice is cooked, add the shrimp and 1 cup of the sauce. Heat thoroughly. Serve the remaining sauce separately.

MAKES SIX ¾-CUP SERVINGS

Each serving contains approximately:
Calories / 227   Cholesterol / 148mg
Fat / 3g   Sodium / 560mg

HAWAIIAN-STYLE CURRIED SHRIMP AND RICE

One 20-ounce can crushed pineapple in its own juice
2 teaspoons curry powder
½ teaspoon salt
½ teaspoon vanilla extract
½ teaspoon coconut extract
One 6-ounce can sliced water chestnuts, drained
3 cups (1 pound) frozen cooked shrimp, thawed
3 cups cooked brown rice

Preheat the oven to 325°F. Combine the pineapple and its juice with the curry powder, salt, and extracts in a large bowl and mix well. Add the water chestnuts, shrimp, and rice and again mix well. Spoon into a 2-quart casserole or baking dish and bake, uncovered, for 30 minutes.

MAKES EIGHT 1-CUP SERVINGS

Each serving contains approximately:
Calories / 191   Cholesterol / 111mg
Fat / 1g   Sodium / 278mg

UPDATED BROCCOLI SEAFOOD CASSEROLE

1 tablespoon corn-oil margarine
3 tablespoons unbleached all-purpose flour
¾ cup defatted chicken stock
½ cup skim milk
½ teaspoon salt (omit if using salted stock)
⅛ teaspoon freshly ground black pepper
⅛ teaspoon garlic powder
⅔ cup light sour cream
2 medium celery ribs, without leaves, chopped (1 cup)
1 medium onion, chopped (1½ cups)
2 tablespoons wheat germ
3 tablespoons dry sherry
¼ pound mushrooms, quartered (2 cups)
½ pound medium shrimp, peeled and deveined
½ pound scallops
2 ounces reduced-fat sharp Cheddar cheese, grated (½ cup)
2 pounds fresh broccoli, peeled and cut into spears

1. Melt the margarine in a medium-size saucepan over medium heat. Add the flour and stir for 1 minute; do not brown. Slowly add the chicken stock and milk and, using a wire whisk, stir until the mixture comes to a boil. Add the salt, pepper, and garlic powder and continue to cook another minute. Remove from the heat.

2. Stir in the sour cream, celery, and onion, then pour the mixture into a shallow 2-quart baking dish sprayed with nonstick vegetable coating and sprinkle with the wheat germ. Spoon the sherry over the top. Bake, uncovered, in a preheated 350°F oven for 35 minutes.

3. Remove from the oven and add the mushrooms, shrimp, and scallops and toss lightly. Sprinkle with the cheese and bake until the seafood is opaque, 10 to 15 minutes.

4. Steam the broccoli over rapidly boiling water until crisp-tender, about 5 minutes. Place on individual plates and spoon ⅔ cup of the seafood over the top of each serving.

MAKES 6 SERVINGS

Each serving contains approximately:
Calories / 250   Cholesterol / 89mg
Fat / 10g   Sodium / 440mg

SEAFOOD IN CREAM SAUCE

2 pounds sea scallops
½ cup defatted chicken stock
½ cup dry vermouth
½ pound mushrooms, sliced
1 cup canned evaporated skimmed milk
1 tablespoon corn-oil margarine
2 tablespoons unbleached all-purpose flour

1. Preheat the oven to 450°F. Bring the scallops, stock, and vermouth to a boil in a large saucepan. Cover and simmer 2 minutes over medium heat. Remove the scallops and add the mushrooms to the liquid. Boil over high heat for 10 minutes. Add the evaporated milk and boil 5 more minutes.

2. Reduce the heat to low, add the margarine and flour and stir with a wire whisk several minutes until thickened. Pour the sauce over the scallops and heat in the oven for 10 minutes.

MAKES FOUR 1-CUP SERVINGS

Each serving contains approximately:
Calories / 294   Cholesterol / 82mg
Fat / 4g   Sodium / 702mg

MARYLAND CRAB CAKES

⅓ cup silken soft tofu
1 teaspoon canola oil
1 teaspoon fresh lemon juice
2 teaspoons reduced-sodium Worcestershire sauce
Pinch each: celery salt, ground white pepper, ground ginger, and paprika
Dash Tabasco sauce or to taste
1 large egg white, lightly beaten
½ cup soft whole-wheat bread crumbs
1½ cups crabmeat (6 ounces), flaked and picked over for cartilage
2 tablespoons finely chopped onion
1 tablespoon finely chopped celery

1. Using a food processor fitted with a metal blade, blend the tofu, oil, lemon juice, Worcestershire sauce, seasonings, and Tabasco sauce until satin smooth. Spoon the mixture into a medium-size bowl, add the remaining ingredients, and mix well. Cover tightly and refrigerate until well chilled.

2. Divide the chilled mixture into twelve 3-ounce patties. Cook in a nonstick skillet over medium heat until brown on both sides. Serve hot.

MAKES 6 SERVINGS

Each serving contains approximately:
Calories / 84   Cholesterol / 26mg
Fat / 2g   Sodium / 175mg

HALIBUT IN COGNAC "CREAM" SAUCE

1 tablespoon corn-oil margarine
1 cup finely chopped onion
1 pound halibut or any other firm white fish, cut into four
    4-ounce fillets
¼ cup cognac or brandy
1 cup low-fat milk, heated to simmering

1. Preheat the oven to 350°F. Melt the margarine in a large skillet over medium heat. Add the onion and cook, stirring, until soft. Add the fish and cook just until lightly browned on each side. Remove the fish from the pan and place in an ungreased baking dish. Bake, uncovered, about 5 minutes. Remove the dish from the oven and cover to keep warm.

2. While fish is baking, pour the cognac or brandy into the hot skillet and stir over medium heat until the pan is almost dry, loosening up any browned bits. Reduce the heat to low, add the milk, mix well, and simmer, covered, for 10 minutes. Remove from the heat, pour into a blender and blend until smooth, then pour through a sieve or a strainer.

3. To serve, place a fish fillet on each of four warm plates and top each with 3 tablespoons of sauce.

MAKES 4 SERVINGS

Each serving contains approximately:
Calories / 200   Cholesterol / 40mg
Fat / 7g   Sodium / 124mg

MONKFISH MEDALLIONS IN LEMON SAUCE

1½ pounds monkfish, sliced into twelve 2-ounce medallions
½ teaspoon salt (omit if using salted stock)
¼ teaspoon freshly ground black pepper
2 tablespoons corn-oil margarine
⅔ cup defatted chicken stock
2 tablespoons sherry
1 tablespoon grated lemon peel
2 tablespoons fresh lemon juice
2 teaspoons cornstarch
1 cup canned evaporated skimmed milk
¼ cup freshly grated Parmesan cheese

1. Place the fish medallions in a plastic bag or between two pieces of waxed paper and flatten slightly with a pan or meat cleaver. Remove from the bag or paper and sprinkle the salt and pepper evenly over the fish. In a large skillet, bring the corn-oil margarine and chicken stock to a boil. Add the fish and cook over medium heat, turning once or twice, just until the fish is opaque, 3 to 5 minutes. Remove the fish from the skillet and place in an ovenproof serving dish.

2. Preheat the broiler. Add the sherry, lemon peel, and lemon juice to the stock and margarine in the skillet. Add the cornstarch to the evaporated milk and mix well with a wire whisk. Gradually add it to the mixture in the skillet, stirring constantly, until the mixture comes to a boil and thickens.

3. Pour the sauce over the fish. Sprinkle the tops of the medallions with Parmesan cheese. Place under the broiler until golden brown, about 2 minutes.

MAKES 6 SERVINGS

Each serving contains approximately:
Calories / 200   Cholesterol / 49mg
Fat / 7g   Sodium / 432mg

SEAWEED STEAMED SALMON ON A BED OF STEAMED VEGETABLES

This recipe uses a technique I learned at the Ritz Cooking School in Paris. You can steam any fish or shellfish over seaweed and then garnish the plates with some of the seaweed for a picture-perfect presentation.

One 2-ounce package dried seaweed
2 medium carrots, cut into thin strips 1½ inches long
1 medium celery root, cut into thin strips 1½ inches long
1 fennel bulb, cut into thin strips 1½ inches long
2 medium zucchini, cut into thin strips 1½ inches long
1 tablespoon extra virgin olive oil
¼ teaspoon salt
¼ teaspoon freshly ground black pepper
1 pound salmon steaks or fillets
2 tablespoons fresh lemon juice
Ground white pepper to taste

1. Place the dried seaweed in a large mixing bowl. Fill the bowl with cool water and set aside to allow the seaweed to reconstitute, about 20 minutes.

2. Steam each vegetable separately until just crisp-tender. Combine the steamed vegetables in a large ovenproof bowl. Add the olive oil, salt, and pepper and mix thoroughly. Cover and place in a warm oven until ready to serve.

3. Drain the seaweed thoroughly and place in a steamer basket. Place the basket over boiling water. Rub the salmon with the lemon juice and lightly sprinkle it with white pepper. Place the fish on top of the seaweed, cover, and steam until opaque, about 5 minutes. Be careful not to overcook.

4. To serve, place a mound of the steamed vegetables in the center of each plate and top with a piece of salmon. The seaweed should be discarded.

MAKES 4 SERVINGS

Each serving contains approximately:
Calories / 300   Cholesterol / 42mg
Fat / 11g   Sodium / 371mg

BROILED SNAPPER ON COUSCOUS

Couscous is a Middle Eastern dish made with cracked semolina wheat. It is very easy to prepare because all you do is add boiling water or stock—there is no cooking required. Therefore, it is used in much the same way we use pasta. I learned this use of couscous with currants at the Ritz Cooking School in Paris.

⅓ cup currants
1⅓ cup uncooked couscous
2 cups water
½ teaspoon salt
One 1-pound red snapper fillet, cut into 4 equal pieces
Freshly ground black pepper to taste
½ cup Herbed Merlot Sauce (see page 28, optional)

1. Cover the currants with warm water and set aside in a small bowl to soften.

2. Preheat the broiler. Put the couscous in a mixing bowl. Combine the water and salt in a small saucepan and bring to a boil. Pour over the couscous and allow to stand until all the water is absorbed. Drain the currants and add to the couscous; mix well. Cover with a lid or a piece of aluminum foil and place in a warm oven until ready to serve.

3. Sprinkle both sides of the fish with a little pepper. Place the fish on an ungreased baking sheet or broiling pan and place under the broiler. Cook only until the fish turns from translucent to opaque, about 4 to 5 minutes. Be careful not to overcook.

4. Spoon ½ cup of the couscous onto the center of each plate. Place a piece of broiled fish on top of the couscous. Top each serving with 2 tablespoons of merlot sauce, if desired.

MAKES 4 SERVINGS

Each serving contains approximately:
Calories / 325   Cholesterol / 40mg
Fat / 2g   Sodium / 345mg

STEAMED RED SNAPPER WRAPPED IN SWISS CHARD

Ann Clark teaches a wonderful weekend cooking class in Austin, Texas, called "Ten Meals to Change Your Life." This recipe was on one of her menus and was a great favorite with the class.

1 tablespoon extra virgin olive oil
1 clove garlic, pressed
Two 8-ounce fresh red snapper fillets, cut into 2 pieces (see
  Note on page 99)

¼ *teaspoon salt*
¼ *teaspoon freshly ground black pepper*
1 *teaspoon grated lemon peel*
2 *medium red bell peppers, seeded and finely diced*
8 *leaves Swiss chard, white rib removed and blanched 1*
    minute, or bok choy, Romaine lettuce, or red or white
    cabbage leaves

1. Combine the olive oil and garlic in a small bowl. Rub each piece of fish with a small amount of the oil and season with salt and pepper. Sprinkle lemon peel and a little red bell pepper on top of each piece of fish, then wrap in two of the blanched Swiss chard leaves.

2. Place on a steamer rack above three inches of boiling salted water, cover tightly, and steam about 8 to 10 minutes per inch of thickness or until opaque all the way through. Remove to a heated platter and serve immediately, or use a bamboo steamer and serve directly from the steamer.

MAKES 4 SERVINGS

Each serving contains approximately:
Calories / 150   Cholesterol / 40mg
Fat / 5g   Sodium / 217mg

NOTE: Redfish, halibut, sea trout, striped bass, sole, salmon fillets, scallops, or shrimp may be substituted for the snapper.

BLACKENED FISH

1 *tablespoon corn-oil margarine*
2 *teaspoons Cajun spices or Cajun Spice Mix (recipe follows)*
One 12½-*ounce can water-packed tuna, drained*

1. Heat a heavy skillet until very hot over very high heat, making sure that the ventilation fan is on. When the skillet is hot, heat the corn-oil margarine until it bubbles. Mix in the spices.

2. Add the tuna and press it down into a flat cake. Allow it to blacken on one side, turn and blacken the other side. Turn once more and remove from skillet. Serve with Cajun rice.

MAKES THREE ⅔-CUP SERVINGS

Each serving contains approximately:
Calories / 190   Cholesterol / 74mg
Fat / 5g   Sodium / 815mg

CAJUN SPICE MIX

1 tablespoon paprika
2½ teaspoons salt
1 teaspoon onion powder
1 teaspoon garlic powder
1 teaspoon cayenne pepper
¾ teaspoon ground white pepper
¾ teaspoon freshly ground black pepper
½ teaspoon dried oregano
½ teaspoon dried thyme

Combine all the spices and mix until well blended. Store, tightly covered, in a cool, dry place.

MAKES 3½ TABLESPOONS

½ teaspoon contains approximately:
Calories / 3   Cholesterol / None
Fat / Negligible   Sodium / 250mg

LIGHT TUNA NOODLE CASSEROLE

6 ounces medium eggless noodles (3½ cups)
One 6½-ounce can water-packed tuna, drained and flaked
¼ cup reduced-calorie mayonnaise
3 large celery ribs, sliced (1 cup)
⅓ cup finely chopped onion
¼ cup diced green bell pepper
One 10-ounce package frozen peas, cooked according to
  package instructions
1 tablespoon corn-oil margarine
1 clove garlic, minced or pressed
3 tablespoons unbleached all-purpose flour
¾ cup defatted chicken stock
½ cup skim milk
½ teaspoon salt (omit if using salted stock)
⅛ teaspoon freshly ground black pepper
2 ounces reduced-fat Cheddar cheese, grated (½ cup)
¼ cup slivered blanched almonds, toasted in a 350°F oven
  until golden brown, 8 to 10 minutes

1. Cook the noodles according to the package directions, omitting salt or oil in the water. Drain and combine in a large bowl with the tuna, mayonnaise, celery, onion, bell pepper, and peas. Set aside.

2. Preheat the oven to 425°F. Melt the margarine in a medium-size skillet. Add the garlic and cook over medium heat just until it starts to sizzle. Add the flour and stir for 1 minute; do not brown. Add the stock and milk and stir with a wire whisk until it comes to a boil. Add the salt and pepper and cook for 1 minute more. Add the cheese and stir until it melts.

3. Pour the sauce mixture into the noodle mixture and mix well. Turn into a 1½-quart casserole and sprinkle with the toasted almonds. Bake until bubbly and slightly crisp on the top, about 20 minutes.

MAKES SIX ⅔-CUP SERVINGS

Each serving contains approximately:
Calories / 327   Cholesterol / 17mg
Fat / 12g   Sodium / 519mg

TUNA TAMALES

FILLING

1 medium onion, finely diced (1½ cups)
1 cup diced raw tuna (8 ounces)
2 tablespoons chopped, drained, canned green chilies
2 tablespoons chopped fresh cilantro
½ teaspoon salt
½ teaspoon freshly ground black pepper

TAMALES

1½ cups masa harina flour (½ pound)
½ teaspoon salt
½ teaspoon freshly ground black pepper
½ teaspoon paprika
¼ teaspoon ground cumin
¼ teaspoon cayenne pepper
¾ cup warm water
2 tablespoons corn oil
1 tablespoon light sour cream

1. To make the filling, cook the onion in a covered medium-size nonstick skillet over medium heat just until soft, about 5 minutes. Add a little water if necessary to prevent scorching. Combine onion with the remaining filling ingredients and mix well. Set aside.

2. To make the tamales, combine the dry ingredients in a medium-size bowl and mix well. Combine the water and oil and add to the dry ingredients, blending until smooth. Mix in the sour cream. Remove from the bowl and knead as you would bread dough until smooth and elastic, about 5 minutes.

3. Divide the dough into six equal balls. Press each ball flat between two pieces of waxed paper and smooth out into a circle 7 inches in diameter with your fingers.

4. Remove the piece of waxed paper on top and place ⅓ cup of the filling mixture in the center of each circle of dough. Using the bottom sheet of paper, lift and fold one edge of the dough over the top of the filling. Repeat with the other edge of the dough to make a tubular envelope and press firmly at the ends to seal the dough tightly around the filling.

5. Roll each tamale in corn husks or plastic wrap and twist each end firmly, tying if necessary to prevent leakage. Steam the tamales over rapidly boiling water for 15 minutes.

MAKES 6 TAMALES

Each tamale contains approximately:
Calories / 195   Cholesterol / 14mg
Fat / 8g   Sodium / 335mg

POULTRY

When cooking poultry, the single most important thing to remember is not to overcook it. If you are roasting a chicken for a meal, put it breast-side down in a flat roasting pan and bake it at 350°F for about 1 hour or until the liquid runs clear when the meat is pierced with a knife. When roasting chicken you are going to allow to cool so that you can chop it to use later as an ingredient, remove it from the oven while the liquid is still running a little bit pink. It will continue to cook as it cools and will give you moister, tastier chicken meat to use in other recipes. If you cook it completely before allowing it to cool, the chicken tends to be dry.

When roasting turkey, wash the turkey inside and out and pat dry. Stuff the turkey with onions, marjoram, and parsley. Using metal skewers, pin the ends of the turkey wings together and close the cavity of the bird. Tie the legs together and place the turkey on its side on a rack in a roasting pan. Pour defatted stock over the top and roast, uncovered, in a preheated 325°F oven for approximately 20 minutes per pound. Baste the bird every 15 to 20 minutes.

Halfway through the cooking, turn the turkey on its other side. If the turkey starts to get too brown, cover it with a lid of foil. Remove the turkey from the oven, transfer it to a platter, and allow it to rest for 20 minutes before carving.

When sautéing chicken breasts it literally takes only a very few minutes per side for the chicken to turn from translucent to opaque and spring back when touched with your finger. At this point they are done, still moist, and very tender.

When working with poultry of any kind it is extremely important not to let it stand out at room temperature. Poultry of all types, as well as eggs, quickly build up harmful bacteria when not refrigerated. This is also true of anything containing poultry or eggs as an ingredient, such as mayonnaise and hollandaise sauce.

When freezing chicken or other poultry, I prefer freezing it with the skin left on. Freezing tends to dehydrate everything, so leaving the skin on helps to protect it.

Chicken, turkey, and rabbit are three of my favorite ingredients because you can use literally any seasoning range with them successfully. You can always substitute one for the other in any recipe and also use them successfully as substitutes for veal.

BREAKFAST PIZZA

1½ cups unbleached all-purpose flour
¼ cup instant nonfat dry milk
1 tablespoon baking powder
¼ teaspoon baking soda
¼ teaspoon salt
3 tablespoons canola oil
⅔ cup buttermilk
1 pound ground turkey sausage
1 cup (5 ounces) peeled and diced potato
4 ounces grated reduced-fat sharp Cheddar cheese (1 cup)
1¼ cups liquid egg substitute
¼ cup skim milk
⅛ teaspoon freshly ground black pepper
2 tablespoons freshly grated Parmesan cheese

1. Mix the flour, dry milk, baking powder, baking soda, and salt in a food processor fitted with a metal blade, or use an electric mixer. Slowly add the oil as machine is running. Scrape the sides of the bowl with a rubber spatula and process again until thoroughly blended.

2. Measure out 2 loosely packed cups of the flour mixture and place in a medium-size bowl, reserving the remaining mix to add if needed. Pour in ⅓ cup buttermilk and beat vigorously. Continue adding the remaining buttermilk and stirring vigorously until a soft dough forms. If the dough is sticky, add a little more dry mix until it is easy to handle.

3. Knead the dough ten times, then press into a 12-inch pizza pan that has been sprayed with nonstick vegetable coating. Press the dough into a thin layer, pushing the excess to the outside edge to form a crust.

4. Preheat the oven to 350°F. Cook the sausage in a large skillet over medium-high heat until golden brown and drain well on paper towels. Boil the potato for 5 minutes in 3 cups water and drain well in a colander. Spread the sausage and potato on top of the dough and sprinkle with the grated Cheddar cheese. In

a small bowl, beat together the egg substitute, milk, and pepper. Pour over the pizza and sprinkle with the Parmesan cheese. Bake until the egg is set and the cheese is melted and golden, about 30 minutes. Cut into wedges and serve immediately.

MAKES 8 SERVINGS

Each serving contains approximately:
Calories / 320   Cholesterol / 46mg
Fat / 13g   Sodium / 560mg

LIGHT DAVENPORT BRUNCH

1 *pound hot turkey sausage*
1 *cup light sour cream*
1 *tablespoon unbleached all-purpose flour*
1 *teaspoon dry mustard powder*
6 *large egg whites, lightly beaten*
2 *ounces reduced-fat sharp Cheddar cheese, grated (½ cup)*

1. Cook the sausage in a medium-size nonstick skillet over medium heat until the sausage is no longer pink, stirring to break up and crumble the sausage. Drain well on paper towels, then place in a medium-size bowl and set aside.

2. Preheat the oven to 325°F. Combine the sour cream, flour, and mustard in a small bowl. Add half this mixture to the cooked turkey sausage and mix well. Spread the turkey mixture in 10-by-6-by-2-inch baking dish sprayed with nonstick vegetable coating.

3. Pour the egg whites evenly over the top of the turkey mixture. Dollop with the remaining sour cream mixture and sprinkle with the grated cheese. Bake until the egg whites look set and are an opaque white, 30 to 40 minutes.

MAKES SIX 1-CUP SERVINGS

Each serving contains approximately:
Calories / 264   Cholesterol / 76mg
Fat / 19g   Sodium / 757mg

LOWER-SODIUM BAKED CHICKEN

2 slices whole-wheat bread, sliced into ¼-inch cubes
2 teaspoons canola oil
¼ teaspoon poultry seasoning
⅛ teaspoon celery seed
⅛ teaspoon onion powder
4 boneless, skinless chicken breast halves (1½ pounds)
Freshly ground black pepper to taste
3 ounces fresh mushrooms, sliced and cooked in a little water
    (¾ cup) or stock over low heat, covered, until tender, about
    5 minutes (1 cup)
¾ cup grated reduced-fat Cheddar cheese (3 ounces)
1 tablespoon corn-oil margarine
3 tablespoons unbleached all-purpose flour
½ cup low-sodium chicken stock
½ cup skim milk
Dash of garlic powder to taste
Dash of freshly ground black pepper to taste

1. Preheat the oven to 300°F. Place the bread cubes in a large shallow pan or on a baking sheet and place in the oven for 20 minutes. Turn a few times so the cubes will brown evenly. Remove from the oven and set aside. Increase the oven temperature to 350°F.

2. In a medium-size bowl, mix together the oil, poultry seasoning, celery seed, and onion powder. Add the bread and toss to coat with the seasonings. Set aside.

3. Place the chicken in a casserole that has been sprayed with nonstick vegetable coating. Sprinkle with freshly ground black pepper and cover with the mushrooms and grated cheese.

4. Melt the margarine in a skillet. Add the flour and stir over medium heat for 3 minutes; do not brown. Add the stock and milk and, using a wire whisk, stir until the mixture comes to a boil. Add the garlic powder and freshly ground black pepper and continue to cook 1 minute more.

5. Pour the sauce over the casserole mixture, then sprinkle the seasoned bread cubes over the top. Bake for 30 minutes, covered. Remove the cover and bake until the chicken is no longer pink, the cheese is melted, and the sauce is hot and bubbly, about 30 minutes more.

MAKES 4 SERVINGS

Each serving contains approximately:
Calories / 384   Cholesterol / 118mg
Fat / 15g   Sodium / 329mg

STUFFING GOOD CHICKEN

8 slices white or whole-wheat bread, cubed and toasted in a
   300°F oven, stirring occasionally, for 20 minutes
4 teaspoons canola oil
½ teaspoon poultry seasoning
¼ teaspoon celery seed
¼ teaspoon onion powder
8 boneless chicken breast halves (2 pounds), skinned and all
   fat removed
6 ounces reduced-fat Swiss cheese slices
1 tablespoon corn-oil margarine
1 clove garlic, minced or pressed
3 tablespoons unbleached all-purpose flour
¾ cup defatted chicken stock
½ cup skim milk
¼ teaspoon salt (omit if using salted stock)
Dash of freshly ground black pepper
¾ cup dry white wine

1. Place the toasted bread cubes in a large bowl. Mix the canola oil, poultry seasoning, celery seed, and onion powder together, then add to the bread and toss to coat evenly.

2. Place the chicken in a 9-by-13-inch baking dish sprayed with nonstick vegetable coating. Cover with a single layer of cheese slices. Spread the seasoned bread cubes on top of the cheese.

3. Preheat the oven to 350° F. In a small, heavy skillet over medium heat, melt the margarine. Add the garlic and cook just until it sizzles. Add the flour and stir for 1 minute; do not brown. Add the stock and milk and, using a wire whisk, stir the mixture until it comes to a boil. Add the salt, pepper, and wine and continue to cook for 1 minute more. Pour the mixture over the chicken and bake for 45 minutes. (May be made the night before, but not baked, to allow the flavors to blend. If refrigerated overnight, allow 5 to 10 more minutes cooking time.)

MAKES 8 SERVINGS

Each serving contains approximately:
Calories / 310   Cholesterol / 82mg
Fat / 10g   Sodium / 341mg

CHICKEN BREASTS IN CHAMPAGNE SAUCE

7 tablespoons unbleached all-purpose flour
¼ teaspoon salt
½ teaspoon freshly ground black pepper
4 boneless chicken breast halves (1 pound), skinned and all fat removed
2 tablespoons plus 2 teaspoons corn-oil margarine
1 pound mushrooms, sliced (6 cups)
1½ cups canned evaporated skimmed milk
½ cup champagne

1. Mix together 4 tablespoons of the flour, the salt, and pepper in a small bowl. Dredge each chicken breast in the mixture and shake off any excess.

2. Melt 2 teaspoons of the margarine in a large, nonstick skillet. Over medium heat, lightly brown the chicken on both sides.

Add the mushrooms, cover, and cook for 5 minutes. Remove the chicken and mushrooms from the skillet with a slotted spoon. Pour off any remaining liquid and wipe the skillet clean.

3. Melt the remaining margarine in the same skillet over low heat. Add the remaining flour and cook for 4 minutes, stirring; do not brown. Remove from the heat and slowly add the milk, stirring constantly with a wire whisk. Return to low heat and cook for 20 minutes, stirring every few minutes (the sauce will be very thick).

4. Add the champagne to the sauce and, stirring constantly with the whisk, cook 5 minutes more. Add the chicken breasts and mushrooms and stir gently until heated through. Good served with rice or pasta.

MAKES 4 SERVINGS

Each serving contains approximately:
Calories / 320   Cholesterol / 53mg
Fat / 10g   Sodium / 414mg

CHICKEN PARISIENNE

4 teaspoons corn-oil margarine
4 tablespoons unbleached all-purpose flour
1 cup defatted chicken stock
¾ cup skim milk
¼ teaspoon salt
Dash of freshly ground black pepper to taste
½ clove garlic, pressed
½ cup plain nonfat yogurt
½ cup sherry
4 chicken breast halves (1 pound), skinned and all fat
* removed*
1 small onion, chopped
1 cup sliced fresh mushrooms

1. Melt the margarine in a medium-size skillet. Add the flour and stir over medium heat for 1 minute; do not brown. Add the chicken stock and milk. Using a wire whisk, stir the mixture until it comes to a boil. Add the salt, pepper, and garlic and continue to cook for 1 minute more.

2. Take off the heat. Combine with the yogurt and sherry. Set aside. Preheat the oven to 400°F.

3. Season the chicken breasts with more freshly ground black pepper. In a large nonstick skillet, brown the chicken on both sides over medium heat. Arrange the chicken, onion, and mushrooms in a baking dish. Pour the sauce mixture over the chicken and vegetables. Bake until hot and bubbly, 30 to 40 minutes. (This is delicious served with rice or pasta.)

MAKES FOUR 1¾-CUP SERVINGS

Each serving contains approximately:
Calories / 296   Cholesterol / 67mg
Fat / 7g   Sodium / 332mg

POACHED BREAST OF CHICKEN WITH CHERVIL CREAM SAUCE

If you are making this dish ahead of time, do not blend the sauce until you have reheated it immediately prior to serving, otherwise it will separate again.

> 1 tablespoon corn-oil margarine
> 3 large leeks, white part only, finely chopped (3 cups)
> 1 pound fresh mushrooms, sliced
> 3 cups defatted chicken stock
> 1 medium onion, quartered
> ½ medium carrot, cut into 1-inch pieces
> 1 large celery rib, cut into 1-inch pieces
> 2 sprigs fresh parsley

3 sprigs fresh thyme or ¼ teaspoon dried, crushed
1 bay leaf, broken
4 boneless chicken breast halves, skinned and all visible fat
 removed
½ cup dry white wine
4 shallots, chopped (¾ cup)
¾ cup canned evaporated skimmed milk
2 tablespoons fresh chervil leaves (see Note below)
¼ teaspoon salt (omit if using salted stock)
⅛ teaspoon freshly ground black pepper
¼ teaspoon fresh lemon juice
16 baby carrots, peeled and steamed for about 4 minutes
8 small red potatoes, peeled and steamed until they can be
 easily pierced with a fork, about 12 minutes

1. Melt the margarine in a heavy pan. Add the leeks and cook, covered, over low heat until soft, about 10 minutes. Add the mushrooms and continue to cook, covered, until the mushrooms are soft, about 5 minutes more. Remove from heat, keep covered, and set aside.

2. Combine the stock, onion, carrot, celery, parsley, thyme, and bay leaf and bring to a boil in a large saucepan. Reduce the heat to medium-low, add the chicken breasts and simmer 4 to 5 minutes. Remove the chicken from the stock and set aside, covered to keep warm.

3. Strain the stock through a colander lined with cheesecloth and discard the vegetables. Return the stock to the pan and bring to a boil. Reduce in volume by one third. While the stock is boiling, combine the wine and shallots and cook over medium heat in a small skillet until the skillet is almost completely dry. Add the reduced stock and bring to a boil. Add the milk and simmer, uncovered, about 30 minutes. Add the chervil, salt, and pepper. (At this point you will think I am completely crazy! The sauce will have separated and looks dreadful.)

4. Pour the sauce into a blender and process until smooth. If the sauce is hot, be sure to leave the lid of the blender slightly ajar to allow steam to escape. (This will prevent the possibility of

hot sauce exploding all over you and your kitchen.) Pour the blended sauce through a sieve or strainer, add the lemon juice and mix well.

5. To serve, divide the mushrooms and leeks equally on four plates (about ¾ cup per plate). Top with a poached chicken breast half and pour ¼ cup sauce over the chicken. Arrange 4 baby carrots and 2 small potatoes decoratively on each plate.

MAKES 4 SERVINGS

Each serving contains approximately:
Calories / 365   Cholesterol / 50mg
Fat / 8g   Sodium / 387mg

NOTE: If chervil is not available, use 1 teaspoon fresh rosemary leaves.

CHICKEN BREASTS IN CURRY SAUCE

This dish is delicious served with rice pilaf and a prepared chutney. If you don't like hot curry, substitute standard curry powder for the Madras curry.

½ cup Madras (hot) curry powder or to taste
⅓ cup unbleached all-purpose flour
6 boneless, skinless chicken breasts, halved
2 tablespoons corn-oil margarine
1 apple, cored and chopped (1 cup)
1 celery rib, without leaves, chopped (½ cup)
1 leek, white part only, chopped (2 cups)
1 medium onion, chopped (1½ cups)
4 cups defatted chicken stock
½ cup dry white wine

1 *cup canned evaporated skimmed milk*
¼ *teaspoon salt (omit if using salted stock)*
4 *ripe bananas, peeled and sliced*
12 *fresh pineapple spears for garnish*

1. Combine the curry powder and flour in a small bowl. Lightly dredge the chicken in the flour mixture and set aside, reserving the leftover flour mixture. Melt 2 teaspoons of the margarine in a large, deep skillet over medium-high heat. Cook half the chicken, turning to brown evenly, until golden. Remove from the skillet and set aside. Melt 2 more teaspoons of the margarine and cook the remaining chicken until golden. Remove from the skillet and set aside. Reduce the heat to medium.

2. Melt the remaining 2 teaspoons margarine in the same skillet and cook the apple, celery, leek, and onion until tender. Stir in the reserved flour mixture and blend well. Add the chicken stock and wine, and bring to a boil, stirring constantly. Reduce the heat to low, and add the chicken. Simmer, covered, until the chicken is no longer pink inside, about 15 minutes. Do not overcook or the chicken will be tough. Remove the chicken to a heated platter and keep warm.

3. Strain the sauce and return it to the skillet. Add the milk and gently bring the sauce to a boil over medium-low heat. Cook the sauce, stirring occasionally, until it is reduced in volume to 2¼ cups. Add the salt and mix well.

4. To serve, place a half breast on each plate. Top with 3 tablespoons sauce and 3 to 4 slices of banana. Garnish with a pineapple spear.

MAKES 12 SERVINGS

Each serving contains approximately:
Calories / 220   Cholesterol / 35mg
Fat / 5g   Sodium / 165mg

CURRIED CHICKEN AND RICE CAKES

½ cup whole-wheat flour
½ teaspoon baking powder
2 cups cooked brown rice
1 cup ground or finely chopped cooked chicken
½ cup finely chopped celery
⅓ cup finely chopped onion
1 tablespoon finely chopped fresh parsley
1 tablespoon reduced-sodium soy sauce
1 tablespoon fresh lemon juice
¾ cup plain nonfat yogurt
1½ teaspoons curry powder
3 large egg whites

1. Preheat the oven to 375°F. In a large bowl, combine the flour and baking powder and mix well. Add all the other ingredients except the egg whites and mix well.

2. Beat the egg whites until stiff but not dry and fold into the chicken-and-rice mixture.

3. Spray twelve standard muffin cups with nonstick vegetable coating and spoon ½ cup of the mixture into each cup. (For larger cakes, use six large muffin cups, spooning 1 cup of the mixture into each.) Bake until golden brown, about 35 minutes. Serve hot.

MAKES 12 CAKES

Each cake contains approximately:
Calories / 77   Cholesterol / 7mg
Fat / 1g   Sodium / 110mg

LIGHT CHICKEN CURRY DIVAN

*4 boned chicken breast halves (about 1 pound), skinned,
cooked, and sliced (about 2 cups) (see page 104)*
*1 pound broccoli, broken into flowerettes and steamed until
crisp-tender, about 5 minutes*
1 tablespoon corn-oil margarine
3 tablespoons unbleached all-purpose flour
¾ cup defatted chicken stock
½ cup skim milk
¼ teaspoon salt (omit if using salted stock)
Dash of garlic powder
Dash of freshly ground black pepper
1 cup crumbled tofu (8 ounces)
1 tablespoon canola oil
1 tablespoon fresh lemon juice
½ teaspoon curry powder
½ cup grated reduced-fat Cheddar cheese
¼ cup plain bread crumbs

1. Preheat the oven to 350°F. Arrange the chicken and broccoli in an ungreased baking dish.

2. Melt the margarine in a medium-size saucepan over medium-low heat. Stir in the flour, and cook 1 minute. Mix the stock and milk together, then gradually add to the flour mixture, stirring constantly with a wire whisk. Continue to cook, stirring, until the mixture thickens.

3. Pour the sauce into a blender or food processor. Add the remaining ingredients, except the cheese and bread crumbs. Blend until smooth. Transfer the sauce back to the saucepan and stir in the cheese.

4. Pour the sauce over the chicken and broccoli and top with the bread crumbs. Bake until bubbly and lightly browned on top, about 30 minutes.

MAKES EIGHT 1-CUP SERVINGS

Each serving contains approximately:
Calories / 182   Cholesterol / 38mg
Fat / 9g   Sodium / 140mg

OVEN CHICKEN AND LINGUINE

2 tablespoons corn-oil margarine
1 medium onion, thinly sliced (2 cups)
2 cloves garlic, minced or pressed
1 tablespoon dried basil, crushed
½ teaspoon crushed red pepper
8 chicken thighs (2½ pounds), skinned
8 ounces uncooked linguine or spaghetti
One pound fresh spinach, veins removed, chopped and
    steamed for 1 minute, or two 10-ounce packages frozen
    chopped spinach, thawed and squeezed dry
2 ounces Parmesan cheese, grated (½ cup)
¼ teaspoon salt
1 small unpeeled orange, quartered

1. Preheat the oven to 400°F. Place the margarine in a 10-by-15-inch baking dish and place the dish in the oven. When the margarine has melted, remove the pan from the oven and stir in the onion, garlic, basil, and red pepper. Roll the chicken pieces in the margarine mixture and leave in the pan. Return the pan to the oven and bake the chicken, uncovered, until the meat near the bone is no longer pink, about 45 minutes.

2. Approximately 10 minutes before the chicken is done, cook the linguine according to the package instructions. Drain. Remove the cooked chicken from the baking dish and keep warm. Add the spinach to the baking dish and stir to scrape the browned bits free. Add the pasta, cheese, and salt, mixing well with two forks.

3. To serve, mound 1½ cups of the pasta mixture on each of four plates. Flank each side with a piece of chicken and place an orange wedge on each plate. Before eating, squeeze orange juice over the chicken and pasta.

MAKES 4 SERVINGS

Each serving contains approximately:
Calories / 810   Cholesterol / 198mg
Fat / 33g   Sodium / 736mg

CHICKEN FETTUCCINE

2 pounds fettuccine, cooked according to package instructions, drained, and cooled
2½ tablespoons corn-oil margarine
½ cup unbleached all-purpose flour
2 cups defatted chicken stock
1¼ cups low-fat milk
5 cloves garlic, chopped
½ teaspoon salt
½ teaspoon ground white pepper
6 ounces Parmesan cheese, grated (1½ cups)
1 pound boneless chicken breast halves, skinned, all fat removed, and cubed
Chopped fresh parsley for garnish

1. Melt the margarine in a medium-size saucepan. Add the flour and stir over medium heat for 1 minute; do not brown. Add the stock, milk, and garlic, and using a wire whisk, stir the mixture until it comes to a boil. Add the salt and pepper and continue to cook for 1 minute more.

2. Slowly add the grated cheese to the sauce, whipping with the wire whisk until the sauce has a creamy consistency.

3. In a large nonstick skillet, cook the chicken over high heat, stirring. Stir and break up pieces. When the outside of the chicken is cooked, drain the water from the skillet and add the sauce. Reduce to medium heat and add the noodles. Stir until hot, 5 to 10 minutes. Be careful not to scorch.

4. Portion out on plates or serve in a casserole dish. Garnish with parsley.

MAKES TWELVE 1½-CUP SERVINGS

Each serving contains approximately:
Calories / 368　　Cholesterol / 33mg
Fat / 8g　　Sodium / 404mg

CHICKEN SCALOPPINE

This recipe is another favorite I found at Ann Clark's cooking class in Austin, Texas. She calls her two-day weekend program "Ten Meals to Change Your Life."

> *4 boneless chicken breast halves, skinned and all fat removed*
> *⅓ cup whole-wheat flour*
> *¼ teaspoon salt*
> *¼ teaspoon freshly ground black pepper*
> *½ teaspoon dried thyme, crushed*
> *2 large egg whites, lightly beaten*
> *½ cup whole-wheat bread crumbs*
> *1 teaspoon grated or finely chopped lemon peel*
> *2 tablespoons fresh lemon juice*
> *2 teaspoons olive oil*
> *Chopped fresh parsley for garnish*
> *Cooked pasta or rice (optional)*

1. One at a time, place each chicken breast between two sheets of waxed paper or in a ziplock bag and, with the flat side

of a meat mallet or heavy spoon, pound evenly to a thickness of ¼ inch.

2. Combine the flour, salt, pepper, and thyme on a dinner plate. Pour the egg whites into a shallow bowl. Combine the bread crumbs and lemon peel on another dinner plate.

3. Rub each breast with the lemon juice, then dredge the chicken breasts, one at a time, in the seasoned flour, dusting off the excess. Dip the floured chicken breasts in the egg whites and then in the bread-crumb mixture.

4. Heat the oil in a large nonstick skillet. Cook the coated chicken breasts over medium-high heat until lightly browned and the meat is no longer pink, about 3 minutes on each side. Serve immediately with a little chopped parsley sprinkled over the top. Serve your favorite pasta or rice on the side if desired.

MAKES 4 SERVINGS

Each serving contains approximately:
Calories / 255   Cholesterol / 73mg
Fat / 6g   Sodium / 329mg

NEW AGE CROQUETTES

1 tablespoon corn-oil margarine
3 tablespoons unbleached all-purpose flour
1 cup skim milk
2 cups finely chopped cooked chicken
1 small onion, finely chopped (½ cup)
¼ teaspoon celery salt
2 teaspoons chopped fresh parsley
1 teaspoon dry mustard
½ cup plain bread crumbs
2 large egg whites, lightly beaten

1. Melt the margarine in a large saucepan over medium-low heat. Add the flour and stir until crumbly. Gradually add the milk and cook until thick, stirring constantly, about 15 minutes.

2. Remove from the heat and add the chicken, onion, and seasonings. Stir until well mixed, then chill for 45 minutes.

3. Preheat the oven to 450°F. Shape the chilled chicken mixture into six cones or cylinders, using about ⅓ cup for each. Roll in the bread crumbs, covering completely, then the egg whites, then the crumbs again. Place on a baking sheet and spray each croquette with nonstick vegetable coating. Bake 15 minutes, then reduce the oven temperature to 350°F and continue baking until the outsides are browned, about 20 minutes.

MAKES 6 CROQUETTES

Each croquette contains approximately:
Calories / 155   Cholesterol / 33mg
Fat / 4g   Sodium / 218mg

BREAST OF CHICKEN TROPICALE

¼ cup orange juice
¼ cup prepared chili sauce
½ teaspoon chili powder
2 tablespoons reduced-sodium soy sauce
2 teaspoons dark sesame oil
1 tablespoon sugar
1 teaspoon grated orange peel
2 cloves garlic, minced or pressed
⅛ teaspoon hot pepper sauce
4 boneless chicken breast halves, skinned, and all fat removed
1 medium orange, thinly sliced

1. Combine the orange juice, chili sauce, chili powder, soy sauce, sesame oil, sugar, orange peel, garlic, and hot pepper sauce in a glass bowl and mix well.

2. Place the chicken in a plastic bag or glass dish. Pour the marinade over the chicken and lay the orange slices on top. Close the plastic bag or cover the dish and marinate for 2 to 4 hours in the refrigerator.

3. Remove from the refrigerator and remove the chicken from the marinade. Pour the marinade into a small saucepan and bring to a boil over medium heat. Reduce heat to low and cook, stirring, for 2 minutes. Set aside. Grill the chicken over medium coals or under a hot broiler about 5 to 6 minutes on each side. Baste with the marinade while the chicken is cooking. Do not overcook.

MAKES 4 SERVINGS

Each serving contains approximately:
Calories / 190   Cholesterol / 66mg
Fat / 5g   Sodium / 630mg

TAMED WILD RICE AND CHICKEN

2 tablespoons corn-oil margarine
½ small onion, chopped
¼ pound fresh mushrooms, sliced
¼ cup unbleached all-purpose flour
1½ cups defatted chicken stock
1½ cups low-fat milk
1 cup wild rice, cooked according to package instructions
3 cups diced cooked skinless chicken breast
One 2-ounce jar pimentos, drained and chopped
2 tablespoons fresh parsley leaves (optional)
½ teaspoon salt (omit if using salted stock)
¼ teaspoon freshly ground black pepper
¼ cup blanched, slivered almonds, toasted in a 350°F oven
  until golden, 8 to 10 minutes

1. Preheat the oven to 350°F. Melt the margarine in large skillet over medium heat. Add the onions and mushrooms and cook until the onions are tender but not brown. Remove from the heat and stir in the flour. Gradually stir in the stock and milk. Return to the heat and stir until the mixture thickens.

2. Add the cooked rice, chicken, pimento, parsley, salt, and pepper. Mix well and place in 2-quart casserole that has been sprayed with nonstick vegetable coating. Sprinkle with the toasted almonds and bake until hot and bubbly, 25 to 30 minutes.

MAKES SIX 1⅓-CUP SERVINGS

Each serving contains approximately:
Calories / 420   Cholesterol / 101mg
Fat / 13g   Sodium / 389mg

"FROM SCRATCH" CHICKEN-AND-RICE CASSEROLE

1 cup brown rice
2 tablespoons corn-oil margarine
6 tablespoons unbleached all-purpose flour
1½ cups defatted chicken stock
1 cup skim milk
1 teaspoon salt (omit if using salted stock)
⅛ teaspoon freshly ground black pepper
1 clove garlic, pressed
½ cup finely chopped fresh mushrooms, placed in a
  microwave-safe bowl lightly covered with waxed paper and
  microwaved on high 1 minute
1 small onion, chopped (1 cup)
½ teaspoon onion powder
2 cups water
8 boneless chicken breast halves (2 pounds), skinned and all
  fat removed

1. Preheat the oven to 350°F. Line a 9-by-13-inch baking dish with aluminum foil. Pour the rice in to cover the bottom.

2. Melt the margarine in a large, heavy skillet over medium heat. Add the flour and stir for 1 minute; do not brown. Add the chicken stock and milk and, using a wire whisk, stir the mixture until it comes to a boil.

3. Add the salt, pepper, garlic, and mushrooms and continue to cook for 1 minute more. Remove from the heat and stir in the onion, onion powder, and water.

4. Pour half of the sauce mixture over the rice. Lay the chicken on top and pour in the remaining sauce mixture. Bake, uncovered, for 2 hours.

MAKES 8 SERVINGS

Each serving contains approximately:
Calories / 260   Cholesterol / 50mg
Fat / 5g   Sodium / 405mg

CHICKEN GO-LIGHTLY CASSEROLE

Six ½-ounce slices Canadian bacon
6 boneless chicken breast halves (1½ pounds), skinned and all fat removed
¼ cup (1½ ounces) dried beef from a package or jar
1 tablespoon corn-oil margarine
1 clove garlic, minced or pressed
¼ cup finely chopped fresh mushrooms
3 tablespoons unbleached all-purpose flour
¾ cup defatted chicken stock
½ cup skim milk
¼ teaspoon salt (omit if using salted stock)
Dash of freshly ground black pepper
½ cup light sour cream
Paprika to garnish

1. Preheat the oven to 300°F. Wrap one slice of bacon around each chicken breast half. Spray an ovenproof casserole with non-stick vegetable coating and cover the bottom with the dried beef. Place the chicken on top. Set aside.

2. In a medium-size skillet over medium heat, melt the margarine. Add the garlic and cook just until it starts to sizzle. Add the mushrooms and cook, stirring, until soft. Add the flour and stir 1 minute; do not brown. Add the chicken stock and milk and, using a wire whisk, stir until the mixture comes to a boil. Add the salt and pepper and continue to cook for 1 minute more. Remove from the heat and stir in the sour cream.

3. Pour the sauce mixture over the chicken and sprinkle with the paprika. Bake until the chicken is no longer pink, the bacon is crisp, and the sauce is hot and bubbly, about 1½ to 2 hours.

MAKES 6 SERVINGS

Each serving contains approximately:
Calories / 200   Cholesterol / 68mg
Fat / 7g   Sodium / 657mg

CHICKEN À LA QUEEN

1 tablespoon corn-oil margarine
⅓ cup chopped mushrooms
¼ cup finely chopped green bell pepper
¼ cup unbleached all-purpose flour
½ teaspoon salt (omit if using salted stock)
⅛ teaspoon freshly ground black pepper
1 cup defatted chicken stock
1 cup canned evaporated skimmed milk
1 cup diced, cooked, skinless chicken breasts
One 2-ounce jar chopped pimentos, drained

1. In a large skillet over low heat, melt the margarine. Add the mushrooms and green pepper and cook, stirring, until the pepper is just crisp-tender. Blend in the flour, salt, and pepper and stir until the vegetables are evenly coated.

2. Remove from the heat and slowly stir in the stock and milk. Return to the heat and bring to a boil, stirring constantly. Boil over medium heat for 1 minute.

3. Add the chicken and pimento and continue stirring until the meat is heated through. Serve hot over toast or noodles.

MAKES FIVE ½-CUP SERVINGS

Each serving contains approximately:
Calories / 144   Cholesterol / 26mg
Fat / 4g   Sodium / 369mg

RITZIER CHICKEN

6 boneless chicken breast halves (1½ pounds), skinned and
   all fat removed
3 large egg whites, lightly beaten
¾ cup seasoned bread crumbs
2 teaspoons olive oil
3 ounces part-skim mozzarella cheese, sliced
1 tablespoon cornstarch
1½ cups canned evaporated skimmed milk
2 ounces Parmesan cheese, grated (½ cup)
2 tablespoons chopped fresh parsley
⅛ teaspoon freshly ground black pepper

1. Dip the chicken breast halves into the beaten egg whites, then dredge in the bread crumbs. Heat 1 teaspoon of the oil in a large frying pan over medium heat. Add half the chicken and brown

lightly on both sides. Remove from the pan and place in a baking dish. Repeat with the remaining oil and chicken. Top the browned chicken with the sliced mozzarella.

2. Preheat the oven to 350°F. Dissolve the cornstarch in 3 tablespoons of the milk. Heat the remaining milk, the Parmesan cheese, parsley, and pepper in a small saucepan over medium heat. Add the cornstarch mixture and cook until the sauce thickens. Pour over the chicken and bake for 25 minutes. Serve immediately. (May be prepared ahead and refrigerated, tightly covered, for a day before baking, if necessary, then bake for 30 minutes.)

MAKES 6 SERVINGS

Each serving contains approximately:
Calories / 331   Cholesterol / 88mg
Fat / 9g   Sodium / 436mg

CHEESE-AND-HERB-STUFFED CHICKEN

3 large egg whites, lightly beaten
1 boneless, skinless chicken breast half, cubed
3 ounces part-skim ricotta cheese
3 ounces chèvre
1 cup grated Parmesan cheese (4 ounces)
¼ cup skim milk
2 scallions, chopped
1 teaspoon dried oregano, crushed
1 ounce sun-dried tomatoes, finely chopped
2 ounces fresh spinach, deveined and chopped (1 cup)
10 boneless, skinless chicken breast halves (2½ pounds)

1. In a food processor, combine the egg whites, cubed chicken, cheese, and milk and process until smooth. Scrape the mixture into a bowl and mix in the scallions, oregano, tomatoes, and spinach. Blend thoroughly and set aside.

2. With a sharp knife, cut a pocket in each chicken breast half to within ½ inch of the sides and end. Do not cut all the way through the small end of the breast.

3. Preheat the oven to 375°F. Fill each pocket with ⅓ cup of the cheese mixture. Arrange the stuffed chicken breasts in a baking dish that has been sprayed with nonstick vegetable coating and bake until the juices from the chicken run clear, about 25 to 30 minutes.

MAKES 10 SERVINGS

Each serving contains approximately:
Calories / 259   Cholesterol / 97mg
Fat / 8g   Sodium / 413mg

HOT TOMATO CASSEROLE

12 corn tortillas
1 tablespoon corn-oil margarine
3 tablespoons unbleached all-purpose flour
¾ cup defatted chicken stock
½ cup skim milk
¼ teaspoon salt (omit if using salted stock)
Dash of freshly ground black pepper
1 clove garlic, pressed
One 10-ounce can Rotel tomatoes, diced
1 pound ground turkey
1 small onion, chopped (½ cup)
4 ounces grated reduced-fat Cheddar cheese (1 cup)

1. Preheat the oven to 350°F. Place the tortillas on two ungreased baking sheets in a single layer. Bake for 10 minutes. Turn the tortillas and bake an additional 3 minutes. Crumble and set aside.

2. While the tortillas are baking, melt the margarine in a medium-size skillet over medium heat. Add the flour and stir for 1 minute. *Do not brown!* Add the stock and milk and, using a wire whisk, stir until it comes to a boil. Add the salt, pepper, and garlic and cook for 1 minute more. Add the tomatoes and mix well. Set aside.

3. In a separate large skillet, brown the turkey and onions over medium-high heat, then drain well. Layer half the crushed tortillas in the bottom of a 2-quart casserole, then spread the turkey mixture evenly over the tortillas, and top with the tomato mixture. Sprinkle the cheese evenly over the top and cover with the remaining tortillas. Bake, uncovered, until bubbly, about 30 minutes.

MAKES SIX 1⅓-CUP SERVINGS

Each serving contains approximately:
Calories / 330   Cholesterol / 72mg
Fat / 15g   Sodium / 442mg

SWISS ENCHILADAS

12 corn tortillas
1 medium onion, chopped (1½ cups)
1 clove garlic, pressed or minced
½ pound lean ground chicken
One 16-ounce can tomato puree (2 cups)
2 canned whole green chilies, chopped (¼ cup)
½ teaspoon salt (omit if using salted stock)
2½ cups defatted chicken stock
2 cups instant nonfat dry milk
½ pound reduced-fat Swiss or Monterey Jack cheese, grated (2 cups)
Fresh cilantro leaves for garnish (optional)

1. Preheat the oven to 350°F. Wrap the tortillas tightly in aluminum foil and place in the preheated oven for 15 minutes to soften.

2. While the tortillas are warming, cook the onions and garlic, covered, in a large saucepan, over low heat until soft, adding a little water or stock if necessary to prevent scorching. Add the chicken and cook over medium heat, stirring frequently until the chicken is cooked, about 5 minutes. Add the tomato puree, chilies, and salt and mix well. Simmer, uncovered, over medium heat, for 10 minutes.

3. While the chicken mixture is simmering, combine the stock and dry milk in a medium-size saucepan and mix thoroughly. Slowly heat to a simmer over medium-low heat, stirring frequently. Dip each tortilla in the milk sauce, then spoon ¼ cup of the chicken mixture down the center.

4. Roll each tortilla around the filling and place, seam-side down, in a glass baking dish that has been sprayed with nonstick vegetable coating. Pour the milk sauce over the top and bake in the oven for 20 minutes. Remove and sprinkle the grated cheese evenly over the top, then return to the oven until the cheese is melted, about 5 minutes.

5. To serve, place each enchilada on a plate and garnish with fresh cilantro, if desired. This recipe may also be made in individual au gratin dishes.

MAKES 12 ENCHILADAS

Each enchilada contains approximately:
Calories / 200   Cholesterol / 25mg
Fat / 4g   Sodium / 278mg

CHICKEN FAJITAS

2 pounds boneless chicken breast halves, skinned, all fat
  removed, and cut into ½-by-3-inch strips
2 medium onions, thinly sliced (4 cups)
¾ cup fresh lime juice
4 cloves garlic, finely chopped
½ teaspoon freshly ground black pepper
1½ teaspoons ground cumin
1 teaspoon dried oregano, crushed
1 medium red bell pepper, cut into thin strips
1 medium green bell pepper, cut into thin strips
Salsa (see page 34)
Fresh cilantro leaves for garnish, optional
12 whole-wheat tortillas, wrapped in aluminum foil and
  warmed in a 300°F oven 8 to 10 minutes

1. Place the chicken and onions in a 9-by-13-inch glass or nonaluminum baking dish. Set aside.

2. Mix together the lime juice, garlic, black pepper, cumin, and oregano. Pour over the chicken and onions, cover and let marinate 2 to 4 hours in the refrigerator, stirring occasionally.

3. Heat a large nonstick skillet over medium-high heat, add the chicken and onions, the bell peppers, and enough of the marinade (1 to 2 tablespoons) to keep the mixture from sticking. Stir-fry just until the chicken becomes opaque and is no longer pink. Do not overcook.

4. Place about ½ cup of the mixture in the center of a warm tortilla. Top with salsa and cilantro, if desired. Fold up the bottom of the tortilla, then fold in the sides to enclose. Eat out of hand accompanied with Cajun Rice (see page 60).

MAKES 12 FAJITAS

Each serving contains approximately:
Calories / 285   Cholesterol / 64mg
Fat / 8g   Sodium / 80mg

EN-LIGHTENED SHIREEN POLLO

6 *teaspoons corn-oil margarine*
3 *medium carrots, thinly sliced (2 cups)*
3 *cups defatted chicken stock*
1 *teaspoon saffron powder or saffron threads pounded into a fine powder*
One *2-ounce package blanched slivered almonds, toasted in a 350°F oven until golden brown, 8 to 10 minutes*
Peel *from 2 medium oranges, white pith discarded and cut in long slivers (½ cup)*
⅓ *cup sugar*
1 *medium onion, thinly sliced (2 cups)*
½ *cup water*
⅛ *teaspoon salt (omit if using salted stock)*
2 *cups long-grain brown rice*
8 *chicken drumsticks (1¾ pounds), skinned*
Freshly *ground white pepper to taste*
2 *tablespoons plus 2 teaspoons finely chopped unsalted pistachio nuts*

1. Heat 1 teaspoon of the margarine in a large, heavy saucepan. Add the carrots and cook over low heat until tender but not brown, stirring occasionally, 8 to 10 minutes. In a small saucepan, heat 1 cup of the stock and stir in the saffron powder. Remove from the heat and let steep 5 minutes. Strain the stock through a colander lined with cheesecloth into the saucepan with the carrots. Add the almonds, orange peel, and sugar. Place over low heat and stir until the sugar has dissolved. Set aside.

2. Melt 4 teaspoons of the margarine in a heavy 2-quart saucepan with a lid. Add the onion and water. Over high heat, cook until the water has boiled away and the onion is soft, 10 to 15 minutes. Add the remaining 2 cups of stock and bring to a boil. Add the salt, rice, and carrot-nut mixture. Mix well, cover tightly, and cook over low heat until all liquid is absorbed, about 1¼ hours.

3. While the rice is cooking, melt the remaining teaspoon of margarine over medium-high heat in a large nonstick skillet with a lid. Brown the drumsticks all over. Sprinkle with white pepper, cover, and cook over low heat for 5 minutes. Turn the drumsticks, cover again, and cook 8 minutes longer. For each serving, spoon 1 cup of the rice mixture onto a plate, top with 1 drumstick, and garnish with 1 teaspoon of the chopped pistachios.

MAKES 8 SERVINGS

Each serving contains approximately:
Calories / 436   Cholesterol / 66mg
Fat / 13g   Sodium / 156mg

MEAT

When buying meat, always look for the leanest cuts available. Currently beef is divided into three grades—select, choice, and prime—depending upon the amount of marbling it contains. The marbling consists of the streaks of fat running through the meat. Select contains the least amount of fat and prime the most.

When preparing meat, always carefully remove all visible fat. Use cooking methods that allow the fat to drain off the meat rather than being held in. For example, when you are baking or broiling meat, always put it on a rack above the pan so the fat is not served with it. When making stews or soups, try to always make them the day before you plan to serve them. Then remove all the visible fat that forms on the top before reheating to serve. This gives you not only a healthier dish but also a more appetizing-looking entrée because it will not have fat globules floating around on top.

The one thing about cooking meat that is much easier than cooking either fish or seafood is that cooking time is not so crucial. Even though there are many cuts of meat that are much better served very rare rather than well done, there are also many others that can be cooked for long periods of time and the time only improves both the taste and the texture.

The single most important tip in preparing and serving meat is to use less of it. Remember that animal protein should never be more than one fifth the volume of your meal. So think in terms of a small steak, a large baked potato, lots of vegetables, and a wonderful salad; or a stir-fry with a little beef, pork, or lamb to add flavor and texture. Treat all meat as a condiment rather than the focus or main part of the meal.

BEST BEEF BOURGUIGNONNE

1½ pounds sirloin steak, cut into 1½-inch cubes
1 cup chopped onion
½ teaspoon onion powder
½ teaspoon salt
1 tablespoon cornstarch
⅔ cup dry red wine
½ pound mushrooms, sliced (2 cups)
½ pound green bell pepper, seeded and cut into 1-inch pieces
*   (1½ cups)*
¾ pound boiling (white pearl) onions, peeled

1. Brown the steak in a nonstick frying pan over medium heat. Combine the onion, onion powder, salt, cornstarch, and wine in a 2-quart casserole. Stir in the steak, mushrooms, bell pepper, and onions.

2. Bake in a preheated 325°F oven until the steak is tender, about 2 hours. Cover for the first hour and uncover the second, stirring several times. Serve with rice.

MAKES SIX ⅔-CUP SERVINGS

Each serving contains approximately:
Calories / 350   Cholesterol / 78mg
Fat / 23g   Sodium / 256mg

BEEF PAPRIKA

2 tablespoons corn-oil margarine
¼ cup sweet Hungarian paprika
1 tablespoon tomato paste
2 pounds lean round steak, cut into 1-inch cubes
½ medium onion, finely chopped (¾ cup)
¾ cup dry red wine
1 cup nonfat sour cream alternative
¼ cup finely chopped fresh dill
½ teaspoon salt
¼ teaspoon cayenne pepper
Chopped fresh dill for garnish

1. Melt the corn-oil margarine in a heavy skillet over low heat. Add the paprika and tomato paste and mix well. Add the beef cubes and cook, stirring, until the meat is well coated. Add the onion and cook, stirring, until tender, about 5 minutes. Add the wine, cover, and simmer until the meat is tender enough to fall off the fork when pierced, about 2 hours.

2. Stir in the sour cream, salt, cayenne pepper, and chopped dill and mix well. Serve immediately. Garnish each serving with a sprinkling of fresh dill. (When reheating, do not allow to boil.)

MAKES FOUR ¾-CUP SERVINGS

Each serving contains approximately:
Calories / 474   Cholesterol / 130mg
Fat / 16g   Sodium / 521mg

LIGHT PEPPER STEAK

1 teaspoon corn-oil margarine
1 clove garlic, minced or pressed
2 pounds very lean beef round steak, cut into strips (2 by ⅛ inches)
1 cup chopped onion
2 small green bell peppers, seeded and cut into strips
One 16-ounce can whole tomatoes, drained
¾ cup defatted beef stock
1 tablespoon cornstarch
¼ cup water
3 tablespoons reduced-sodium soy sauce
1 teaspoon sugar
¼ teaspoon salt (omit if using salted stock)

1. Melt the margarine in a large skillet over medium heat. Add the garlic and cook just until it begins to sizzle; do not brown. Add the beef strips and cook, stirring occasionally, until browned.

2. Remove the meat from the skillet. Add the onion and bell peppers and cook, stirring, about 2 minutes, adding a little water or stock, if needed, to prevent scorching.

3. Return the meat to the skillet and add the drained tomatoes and beef stock. Simmer for 5 minutes over medium heat.

4. While the skillet mixture is simmering, blend together the cornstarch, water, soy sauce, sugar, and salt. Stir into the meat mixture and cook, stirring, until thickened, about 10 to 15 minutes. Serve at once with whipped potatoes or rice.

MAKES SIX 1-CUP SERVINGS

Each serving contains approximately:
Calories / 256   Cholesterol / 86mg
Fat / 7g   Sodium / 435mg

LIGHT STROGANOFF

1 tablespoon corn-oil margarine
1 clove garlic, minced or pressed
3 tablespoons unbleached all-purpose flour
½ cup skim milk
¾ cup defatted beef or chicken stock
¼ teaspoon salt (omit if using salted stock)
¼ teaspoon freshly ground black pepper
1 tablespoon canola oil
1 clove garlic, finely chopped
½ cup finely chopped onion
1½ pounds lean round steak, trimmed of all fat and sliced in
thin strips
½ pound fresh mushrooms, sliced
1 cup nonfat sour cream alternative
Finely chopped parsley for garnish

1. In a medium-size saucepan, melt the margarine over medium heat. Add the minced or pressed garlic and cook just until it sizzles. Add the flour and cook, stirring with a wire whisk for about 1 minute; do not brown. Add the milk, stock, salt, and pepper. Continue stirring with the whisk until the mixture thickens and comes to a boil. Remove from the heat and set aside.

2. Heat the oil in a large nonstick skillet over medium heat. Add the chopped garlic, onion, and beef strips and cook, stirring, until the onion is soft and the meat is browned. Add the mushrooms, cover, and cook over low heat for 15 minutes. Uncover, add the sauce mixture, and continue to cook until the meat is tender, about 30 to 40 minutes.

3. Stir in the sour cream, mix well, and cook until heated through. Serve over noodles or rice, garnished with parsley.

MAKES FOUR 1-CUP SERVINGS

Each serving contains approximately:
Calories / 376   Cholesterol / 98mg
Fat / 14g   Sodium / 342mg

YECCA

1 cup skim milk
2 tablespoons unbleached all-purpose flour
2 teaspoons sugar
1 teaspoon salt
¼ teaspoon freshly ground black pepper
Pinch of cayenne pepper
2 cups fresh or frozen corn kernels, thawed
1 medium onion, chopped (1½ cups)
1 clove garlic, minced or pressed
1 pound ground turkey
½ pound extra-lean ground beef
One 8-ounce can tomato sauce
1 small green bell pepper, seeded and chopped
8 ounces reduced-fat sharp Cheddar cheese, grated
1 teaspoon fresh lemon juice
2 large egg whites, lightly beaten

1. In a large saucepan, combine the milk, flour, sugar, salt, and black and cayenne peppers. Cook over medium heat until thick, stirring often, about 25 minutes. Add the corn, onion, and garlic, then pour the mixture into a blender container and puree until smooth.

2. Brown the turkey and beef in a large skillet over medium-high heat just until the meat loses its pink color. Drain off any fat, remove from the heat, and add the pureed corn mixture, tomato sauce, bell pepper, all but ½ cup of the grated cheese, the lemon juice, and egg whites. Mix well and pour into a 9-by-13-inch glass baking dish or casserole that has been sprayed with nonstick vegetable coating.

3. Sprinkle with the remaining cheese and bake in preheated 350°F oven until the cheese is melted and the mixture is set, about 1 hour.

MAKES SIX 1¼-CUP SERVINGS

Each serving contains approximately:
Calories / 425   Cholesterol / 111mg
Fat / 22g   Sodium / 653mg

"HEARTY" HAMBURGER PIE

1 pound extra-lean ground round
1 medium onion, chopped (1½ cups)
1 clove garlic, minced or pressed
1 teaspoon sugar
¼ teaspoon salt
⅛ teaspoon freshly ground black pepper
½ pound fresh green beans, sliced into 1-inch pieces, steamed
   5 minutes, rinsed with cold water, and drained
One 6-ounce can unsalted tomato paste
½ cup tomato sauce
1½ pounds (5 medium) Russet potatoes, peeled, quartered,
   cooked in boiling water until tender, 15 to 20 minutes,
   drained
½ cup skim milk, warmed
1 large egg white, lightly beaten
⅛ teaspoon salt
Dash of freshly ground black pepper to taste
2 ounces reduced-fat sharp Cheddar cheese (½ cup; optional)

1. In a large nonstick skillet, lightly brown the meat over medium-high heat and drain thoroughly. Return the meat to the skillet and add the onion and garlic. Reduce the heat to low and cook until the onion is tender, about 8 to 10 minutes. Add the sugar, the salt, the pepper, steamed beans, tomato paste, and tomato sauce. Mix well.

2. Pour the mixture into a 1½-quart casserole sprayed with

nonstick vegetable coating. Mash the potatoes with the milk, egg white, the remaining salt, and a dash of pepper. Drop in mounds over the meat mixture and sprinkle with the grated cheese, if desired.

3. Bake in a preheated 350°F oven until the potatoes are golden and the casserole is hot and bubbly, about 25 to 30 minutes.

MAKES 4 SERVINGS

Each serving contains approximately:
Calories / 365   Cholesterol / 65mg
Fat / 5g   Sodium / 650mg

ITALIAN MEAT PIE

¾ pound extra-lean ground beef
½ cup chopped onion
1 small green bell pepper, seeded and chopped (½ cup)
1 clove garlic, minced or pressed
2 teaspoons cornstarch
¾ cup water
One 6-ounce can tomato paste
½ teaspoon dried oregano, crushed
½ teaspoon dried basil, crushed
¼ teaspoon salt
⅛ teaspoon freshly ground black pepper
⅓ cup freshly grated Parmesan cheese
One 9-inch frozen deep-dish pie shell
4 ounces grated part-skim mozzarella cheese (1 cup)

1. Preheat the oven to 400°F. In a large nonstick skillet, brown the beef over medium heat and drain well. Add the onion, bell pepper, and garlic and cook, stirring, 5 minutes. Dissolve the cornstarch in the water and add to the skillet along with the tomato paste and all the seasonings. Cover and simmer 10 minutes.

2. Sprinkle half of the Parmesan cheese over the bottom of the frozen pie shell. Cover with half of the meat mixture, then half of the mozzarella. Layer with the remaining meat and the Parmesan cheese. Bake on a cookie sheet for 15 minutes. Sprinkle with the mozzarella and return to oven until the cheese melts, about 5 more minutes.

MAKES 6 SERVINGS

Each serving contains approximately:
Calories / 310   Cholesterol / 50mg
Fat / 16g   Sodium / 415mg

MEAT LOAF

1 teaspoon corn-oil margarine
1 cup finely chopped onions
2 cloves garlic, minced
3 slices whole-wheat bread
1 cup skim milk
2 pounds very lean ground beef
3 large egg whites, lightly beaten
1 teaspoon salt
¼ teaspoon freshly ground black pepper
¼ cup finely chopped fresh parsley
¾ teaspoon dried thyme, crushed
¾ teaspoon dried marjoram, crushed
One 6-ounce can tomato paste

1. Preheat the oven to 375°F. Spray a 13-by-9-inch baking dish with nonstick vegetable coating.

2. Melt the margarine in a medium-size skillet, add the onion and garlic and cook, stirring frequently, until just golden; do not brown. Set aside.

3. Remove the crusts from the bread. Place the crusts in a blender and process on high to make fine bread crumbs. Set aside. Dice the remaining bread into ½-inch cubes and soak in the milk.

4. In a large mixing bowl, combine the beef, onion mixture, and bread cubes by hand. Stir in all remaining ingredients except the tomato paste and reserved bread crumbs, and mix by hand in a circular motion, forming the meat into a ball.

5. Place a rack in the pan and put the meat mixture on the rack. Pat the meat into a loaf shape, leaving at least 1 inch of space around the edges to allow fat to run off.

6. Spread the tomato paste on top of the meat and sprinkle the reserved bread crumbs on top. Cover with aluminum foil or plastic wrap and refrigerate for 1 hour to allow the flavors to blend and to firm up the loaf.

7. Bake on the lower shelf of the oven until the meat is cooked through, about 1 hour. Pour off the accumulated fat after the meat is fully cooked. Let stand for 5 minutes before slicing.

MAKES 8 SERVINGS

Each serving contains approximately:
Calories / 330   Cholesterol / 94mg
Fat / 17g   Sodium / 634mg

HEALTHY BBQ MEAT LOAF

1½ pounds extra-lean ground beef
1½ cups soft whole-wheat bread crumbs (about 3 slices
*   ground in a blender or food processor)*
2 large egg whites
½ cup chopped onion
½ teaspoon salt
¼ teaspoon freshly ground black pepper
1¾ cups tomato sauce

2 *tablespoons Worcestershire sauce*
3 *tablespoons prepared mustard*
3 *tablespoons vinegar*
½ *cup frozen unsweetened apple juice concentrate, thawed*

1. Preheat the oven to 350°F. Combine the meat, bread crumbs, egg whites, onion, salt, pepper, 1 cup of the tomato sauce, and 1 tablespoon of the Worcestershire sauce in a large bowl. Shape into a loaf and place in a 7-by-11-inch baking dish. Cover with aluminum foil and bake 45 minutes. Remove from the oven and pour off any fat that has accumulated in the pan.

2. Combine the remaining tomato sauce and Worcestershire sauce, the mustard, vinegar, and apple juice concentrate in a small bowl. Pour over the meat loaf. Continue to cook, uncovered, until the sauce is hot and bubbly, about 15 minutes more, basting every 5 minutes. Let rest about 5 minutes before slicing. Good served hot or cold.

MAKES 8 SERVINGS

Each serving contains approximately:
Calories / 215   Cholesterol / 65mg
Fat / 5g   Sodium / 675mg

SPINACH HASH

1 *pound extra-lean ground beef*
1 *tablespoon extra virgin olive oil*
1 *medium onion, chopped (1½ cups)*
1 *pound fresh spinach, well washed, stems removed, deveined, and chopped*
3 *large egg whites*
½ *teaspoon salt*
¼ *teaspoon freshly ground black pepper or to taste*

1. Put the ground beef in a heavy skillet and cook over medium-high heat about 3 minutes, breaking up the meat with a spoon and stirring to assure even browning. Add the olive oil, onions, and spinach and cook, stirring occasionally, until the onions are tender, about 5 to 7 minutes.

2. Combine the egg whites, salt, and pepper and beat until well mixed. Pour the egg whites into the skillet and stir until all the moisture is absorbed. Serve hot.

MAKES 4 SERVINGS

Each serving contains approximately:
Calories / 307   Cholesterol / 74mg
Fat / 20g   Sodium / 425mg

BAYFIELD EGGS

2 cups liquid egg substitute
1 pound ground turkey sausage
8 ounces reduced-fat sharp Cheddar cheese, grated (2 cups)
1 cup finely chopped onion (½ large onion)
¾ cup finely chopped green bell pepper
2 cups sliced mushrooms
½ teaspoon freshly ground black pepper
1 cup canned evaporated skimmed milk

1. Pour the liquid egg substitute into the bottom of a lightly greased 9-by-13-inch glass baking dish.

2. Cook the sausage in a nonstick skillet over medium-high heat until lightly browned, breaking the sausage apart into small pieces. Drain well on paper towels. Cover the egg substitute evenly with the sausage.

3. Top the sausage with half of the grated cheese. Layer the onion, bell pepper, and then the mushrooms on top of the cheese. Sprinkle with the black pepper. Pour the evaporated milk evenly over all. Top with the remaining cheese. Refrigerate, tightly covered, overnight.

4. Bake in a preheated 350°F oven until the top is lightly browned and the egg substitute looks firm, 40 to 45 minutes. Remove from the oven and let rest 5 minutes before serving.

MAKES 8 SERVINGS

Each serving contains approximately:
Calories / 240   Cholesterol / 60mg
Fat / 8g   Sodium / 410mg

HAM AND CHEESE STRATA

Twelve 1-ounce slices French bread
3 ounces extra-lean cooked ham, thinly sliced
3 ounces reduced-fat Cheddar cheese, thinly sliced
1 cup liquid egg substitute
½ teaspoon salt
1 teaspoon dry mustard
4 cups skim milk
3 ounces reduced-fat Cheddar cheese, grated (¾ cup)
Paprika

1. Spray a 9-by-13-inch glass baking dish with nonstick vegetable coating. Make six sandwiches with bread, ham, and sliced cheese. Place in the dish.

2. Combine the egg substitute, salt, mustard, and milk, and pour over the sandwiches. Sprinkle with the grated cheese and paprika. Let stand 1 hour or place in the refrigerator overnight.

3. Bake in a preheated 350°F oven until the cheese is melted and the sandwiches are a golden brown, about 1¼ hours. Serve immediately.

MAKES 6 SERVINGS

Each serving contains approximately:
Calories / 370   Cholesterol / 37mg
Fat / 11g   Sodium / 957mg

TURKEY HAM AND BRIE PASTA

12 ounces rotini or rotelle
One 9-ounce package frozen French-cut green beans
2 tablespoons corn-oil margarine
¼ cup unbleached all-purpose flour
2 cups skim milk
¼ cup dry white wine
4 ounces Brie, rind removed, cut into chunks
2 ounces reduced-fat Monterey Jack cheese, shredded (½ cup)
½ pound thinly sliced turkey ham, cut into thin strips

1. Cook the pasta according to package directions, adding the green beans during the last 2 minutes of cooking.

2. Meanwhile, in a medium-size saucepan, melt the margarine. Stir in the flour and cook 2 minutes over medium heat, stirring constantly; do not brown. Gradually add the milk and bring to a boil, whisking until smooth. Add the wine and boil for 1 minute, whisking constantly until the sauce thickens. Reduce the heat to low and gradually add the cheeses, whisking after each addition until melted. Keep the sauce warm, stirring occasionally.

3. Drain the pasta and beans and place in large serving bowl. Add the turkey ham and toss, then add the cheese sauce and continue tossing until well coated. Serve hot.

PEPPER, CHEESE, HAM, RICE QUICHE

CRUST

2½ cups cooked brown rice, warm
4 tablespoons (½ stick) corn-oil margarine, melted

FILLING

4 ounces reduced-fat Cheddar cheese, shredded
¾ teaspoon Tabasco sauce
One 2-ounce jar pimentos, drained and diced
4 ounces reduced-fat Swiss cheese, shredded
3 ounces extra-lean cooked ham, finely diced (½ cup)
4 large egg whites
½ cup low-fat milk
⅛ teaspoon paprika
Dash of garlic powder
Dash of onion powder

1. Spray a 9-inch pie pan with nonstick vegetable coating. Use the back of a large spoon to press the rice over the pie pan to form the crust. Brush with the melted margarine. Place a pre-heated 350°F oven for 2 to 3 minutes to let the margarine soak into the rice. Remove from the oven and set aside.

2. Combine the Cheddar cheese, Tabasco and pimentos in a medium-size bowl. Add the Swiss cheese and ham and mix well. Fill the rice crust with the cheese-and-ham mixture.

3. In another bowl, beat together the egg whites, milk, pa-

prika, garlic powder, and onion powder. Pour over the other ingredients evenly. Bake at 350°F until a knife inserted in the center comes out clean, 30 to 40 minutes.

MAKES 6 SERVINGS

Each serving contains approximately:
Calories / 317   Cholesterol / 35mg
Fat / 17g   Sodium / 620mg

SPAGHETTI ALLA CARBONARA

¼ pound Canadian bacon, chopped
2 tablespoons corn-oil margarine
1 tablespoon extra virgin olive oil
½ teaspoon dried red pepper flakes
1 large egg and 2 large egg whites, lightly beaten
½ cup canned evaporated skimmed milk
⅓ cup plus 3 tablespoons freshly grated Parmesan cheese
12 ounces spaghetti

1. Warm a serving bowl in a 200°F oven. In a nonstick skillet, cook the bacon until slightly browned. Remove the bacon from the skillet and set aside. In the same skillet, heat the margarine and olive oil over very low heat. When the margarine is melted, add the red pepper flakes and, stirring continuously with a wire whisk, the beaten egg mixture. As the sauce begins to thicken, stir in the milk and ⅓ cup of the cheese. Keep warm over very low heat, stirring frequently. (It is important the heat be very low or you may end up with scrambled eggs!)

2. Boil the spaghetti in a large kettle of boiling water for about 7 minutes. Do not overcook. Drain well and place in the preheated bowl. Working quickly, toss the spaghetti with the sauce and bacon and serve at once in heated bowls. Sprinkle each serving with 1½ teaspoons of the Parmesan cheese.

MAKES EIGHT ¾-CUP SERVINGS

Each serving contains approximately:
Calories / 270   Cholesterol / 38mg
Fat / 8g   Sodium / 340mg

LIGHT MANICOTTI

¾ *pound extra-lean cooked ham*
2 *ounces reduced-fat Swiss cheese, grated (½ cup)*
2 *ounces part-skim mozzarella cheese, grated (½ cup)*
2¾ *cups skim milk*
1 *large egg and 2 large egg whites, beaten together*
2 *tablespoons plain bread crumbs*
¼ *teaspoon freshly ground black pepper*
12 *manicotti, cooked according to package instructions,*
  drained
1 *tablespoon corn-oil margarine*
3 *tablespoons unbleached all-purpose flour*
⅛ *teaspoon salt*
1 *ounce Parmesan cheese, freshly grated (¼ cup)*

1. To make the filling, process the ham in a food processor or meat grinder until finely ground. Add the cheeses, ¼ cup of the milk, the eggs, bread crumbs, and pepper. Mix well and fill each manicotti with ¼ cup filling, using either a decorator gun or spoon.

2. To make the sauce, bring the remaining milk to a simmer over low heat. In a separate saucepan, melt the margarine over low heat. Add the flour and cook for 2 minutes, stirring constantly; do not brown. Remove from the heat and slowly add the simmering milk, stirring with a wire whisk. Add the salt and a dash of pepper and cook over low heat, stirring occasionally, until thickened, 15 to 20 minutes.

3. Spray a 9-by-13-inch baking dish with nonstick vegetable coating. Spoon in a little sauce to cover the bottom. Add the manicotti and then pour the sauce over them, and top with the Parmesan cheese. Bake in a preheated 350°F oven until very hot, about 25 minutes.

MAKES 6 SERVINGS

Each serving contains approximately:
Calories / 353   Cholesterol / 68mg
Fat / 10g   Sodium / 934mg

FETTUCCINE WITH PEAS AND HAM

1 tablespoon plus 1 teaspoon corn-oil margarine
¼ pound shallots, minced (¼ cup)
½ pound fresh mushrooms, sliced (2 cups)
3 tablespoons unbleached all-purpose flour
2 cups skim milk, heated to simmering
⅛ teaspoon salt
One 10-ounce package frozen tiny peas, thawed
¼ pound extra-lean ham, chopped
1 pound fettuccine, cooked according to package instructions
1 cup (4 ounces) freshly grated Parmesan cheese
Freshly ground black pepper to taste

1. In a large saucepan over medium heat, melt 1 teaspoon of the margarine. Add the shallots and cook until soft, stirring occasionally. Add the mushrooms, increase the heat to high, and cook, stirring occasionally, until the mushrooms are very lightly browned. Remove the vegetable mixture from the saucepan and set aside.

2. In the same pan, melt the 1 tablespoon margarine over low heat. Add the flour and cook for 3 minutes, stirring constantly.

Do not brown. Remove from the heat and slowly add the milk, stirring constantly with a wire whisk. Stir in the salt, return to low heat, and cook for 15 to 20 minutes, stirring occasionally. Add the peas and cook 30 seconds longer.

3. In a large serving bowl, combine the sauce, vegetable mixture, ham, fettuccine, and ¾ cup of the cheese. Toss until the sauce clings to the pasta. Season to taste with a generous amount of freshly ground black pepper. Sprinkle each serving with 1½ teaspoons cheese.

MAKES EIGHT 1¼-CUP SERVINGS

Each serving contains approximately:
Calories / 354   Cholesterol / 13mg
Fat / 7g   Sodium / 475mg

BAKED HAM AND VEAL LOAF

LOAF

1 pound extra-lean cooked ham, ground or very finely
  chopped
1½ pounds extra-lean ground veal
½ cup liquid egg substitute
1 cup skim milk
1 cup soft whole-wheat bread crumbs (1½ slices crumbled in
  a blender)
⅛ teaspoon freshly ground black pepper
6 slices canned pineapple

SAUCE

½ cup firmly packed dark brown sugar
1 teaspoon dry mustard
¼ cup white vinegar

1. Mix together the meats, egg substitute, milk, crumbs, and pepper in a large bowl. In a separate bowl, combine the sauce ingredients.

2. Spray a large loaf pan with nonstick vegetable coating. Place the pineapple slices on the bottom of the pan and pour half the sauce mixture over them.

3. Pack the meat mixture over the fruit and sauce. Pour the remaining sauce over the top of the loaf. Bake in a preheated 400°F oven until hot and bubbly, 1½ to 2 hours. Turn out onto a platter and serve.

MAKES 8 SERVINGS

Each serving contains approximately:
Calories / 338   Cholesterol / 83mg
Fat / 11g   Sodium / 840mg

PASTITSIO

MEAT MIXTURE

2 small onions, chopped (2 cups)
1 pound very lean ground lamb
One 16-ounce can whole tomatoes, drained and mashed
One 8-ounce can tomato sauce
½ teaspoon salt
½ teaspoon dried oregano, crushed
¼ teaspoon ground cinnamon
⅛ teaspoon freshly ground black pepper
1 slice whole-wheat bread, toasted and crumbled (½ cup)

WHITE SAUCE

3 tablespoons corn-oil margarine
⅓ cup unbleached all-purpose flour
2½ cups skim milk, heated to simmering

½ *teaspoon salt*
¼ *teaspoon ground cinnamon*
⅛ *teaspoon ground white pepper*
3 *large egg whites, lightly beaten*
½ *cup part-skim ricotta cheese*
1 *pound elbow macaroni or tube-shaped pasta, cooked*
  according to package instructions
4 *ounces Romano cheese, grated (1 cup)*

1. In a large covered saucepan over low heat, cook the onion until soft, adding a little water if necessary to prevent scorching. Add the lamb and cook until done, about 5 minutes. Add the crushed tomatoes, tomato sauce, and seasonings. Mix well, cover, and simmer 40 minutes, stirring occasionally. Add the bread crumbs and mix well.

2. While the mixture is cooking, make the sauce. Melt the margarine in a medium-size skillet over medium heat. Add the flour and cook 3 minutes, stirring constantly. Be careful not to brown the flour. Add the simmering milk, stirring constantly until smooth. Add the salt, cinnamon, and pepper and cook, stirring frequently, until thickened. Remove from the heat and slowly add the egg whites, stirring constantly. Combine 1 cup of the sauce with the ricotta cheese, mix well, and set aide.

3. To assemble, preheat the oven to 350°F. Spray a 9-by-13-inch baking dish with nonstick vegetable coating. Spread half the cooked macaroni in the dish and top with the meat mixture. Pour the white sauce without the cheese evenly over the top. Sprinkle half the grated Romano cheese over the top. Cover with the remaining macaroni and bake for 30 minutes.

4. Remove from the oven and increase the oven temperature to 400°F. Spread the reserved cheese and sauce mixture over the top and sprinkle evenly with the remaining Romano cheese. Bake until slightly browned, another 20 to 30 minutes. Cool 10 minutes before serving.

MAKES EIGHT 1½-CUP SERVINGS

Each serving contains approximately:
Calories / 483   Cholesterol / 64mg
Fat / 12g   Sodium / 752mg

MALAYSIAN PORK SATAY

When I was in Malaysia attending the eighth annual Asian Conference on Nutrition I became enamored with the many varieties of Malaysian satay.

2 tablespoons unhomogenized peanut butter
½ cup minced onion
1 clove garlic, minced
2 tablespoons fresh lemon juice
2 tablespoons soy sauce
1 tablespoon packed brown sugar
2 teaspoons dark sesame oil
Dash of hot pepper sauce to taste
1 pound boneless pork loin, all visible fat removed, cut into
¾-inch cubes

1. Put all the ingredients except the pork in a blender and process until smooth. Combine the pork and marinade in a large bowl. Cover and let the pork marinate for at least 30 minutes in the refrigerator.

2. Remove the pork from the marinade and thread the pork on skewers (if using bamboo skewers, soak them in water for 1 hour to prevent burning). Grill over hot coals or broil under a preheated broiler, turning occasionally, until evenly brown on all sides, 10 to 12 minutes. Serve with hot cooked rice if desired.

MAKES 4 SERVINGS

Each serving contains approximately:
Calories / 155   Cholesterol / 40mg
Fat / 10g   Sodium / 294mg

MEXICAN CASSEROLE

1 tablespoon corn-oil margarine
1 clove garlic, minced or pressed
¼ cup finely chopped mushrooms
¼ cup unbleached all-purpose flour
¾ cup defatted chicken stock
½ cup skim milk
1 teaspoon salt (omit if using salted stock)
⅛ teaspoon freshly ground black pepper
One 8-ounce can tomato sauce
¼ teaspoon sugar
1 teaspoon chili powder
¼ teaspoon paprika
Dash of cayenne pepper
½ pound extra-lean ground beef
1 large onion, chopped
1 dozen corn tortillas, torn into pieces
8 ounces reduced-fat sharp Cheddar cheese, grated

1. Melt the margarine in a small saucepan over medium heat. Add the garlic and cook just until it starts to sizzle, then add the mushrooms and cook, stirring, until tender, about 5 minutes. Add 3 tablespoons of the flour and stir for 1 minute. Do not brown. Slowly add the stock and milk. Using a wire whisk, stir the mixture until it comes to a boil. Add the salt and pepper and continue to cook 1 minute more. Set aside.

2. In a small bowl, combine the tomato sauce, sugar, the remaining flour, chili powder, paprika, and cayenne pepper. Add this mixture to the mushroom sauce and stir well with a wire whisk.

3. Brown the beef and onion in a large nonstick skillet over medium heat, drain the liquid, then add the sauce mixture and mix well. Spray a 9-by-13-inch baking pan with nonstick vegetable coating. Layer half the tortilla pieces in the bottom, then half the meat mixture, then half the cheese. Repeat the layers and bake in a preheated 350°F oven until the cheese is melted and the tortillas are crisp, 35 to 45 minutes.

MAKES SIX 1-CUP SERVINGS

Each serving contains approximately:
Calories / 414   Cholesterol / 61mg
Fat / 19g   Sodium / 940mg

MOUSSAKA (GREEK EGGPLANT CASSEROLE)

MEAT FILLING

1 teaspoon olive oil
1 pound lean ground lamb or extra-lean ground beef
1 small onion, chopped
2 cloves garlic, crushed
½ cup tomato paste
1 cup dry white wine
½ cup water
½ teaspoon ground cinnamon
½ cup chopped fresh parsley
½ teaspoon salt
½ teaspoon freshly ground black pepper

EGGPLANT PREPARATION

2 medium eggplants (2 pounds)
Salt

BÉCHAMEL SAUCE TOPPING

3 cups skim milk
½ teaspoon salt
¼ teaspoon freshly grated nutmeg
⅓ cup uncooked Cream of Rice cereal

½ cup Parmesan cheese, grated
½ teaspoon ground cinnamon

1. Heat the oil in a large skillet over medium-high heat. Cook the meat and onion until the meat is no longer pink. Add the remaining filling ingredients and simmer for 10 minutes. Set aside.

2. Peel the eggplant and cut into ½-inch rounds. Lay the slices on a large baking sheet or tray. Lightly sprinkle both sides of the eggplant with salt and let stand at room temperature for 30 minutes. Rinse the eggplant under cold running water to remove the salt and dry thoroughly with paper towels.

3. Steam the eggplant slices until fork tender, about 5 minutes. Drain on paper towels to remove any moisture. Set aside.

4. Bring all the béchamel sauce ingredients, except the Cream of Rice, to a boil in a small saucepan. Add the Cream of Rice and stir for 1 minute. Remove from the heat, cover, and allow to stand for 5 minutes.

5. Pour the mixture into a blender and process until smooth. Set aside.

6. Preheat the oven to 325°F. Spray a 13-by-9-inch baking dish or casserole with nonstick vegetable coating. Cover the bottom with half the eggplant slices. Spread all of the meat filling over the eggplant. Top with the remaining half of the eggplant slices. Spread the béchamel sauce over the top and sprinkle with the Parmesan cheese and ground cinnamon.

7. Bake until béchamel sauce is set, 45 minutes. Cool 5 minutes, then cut into squares and serve.

MAKES 8 SERVINGS

Each serving contains approximately:
Calories / 297   Cholesterol / 48mg
Fat / 14g   Sodium / 475mg

BREADS

Bread is truly the staff of life, and the staff is stronger when breads are made from whole grains. More than a third of the world's population gets its daily calories from wheat alone.

Wheat, although it is the most popular and most often used grain, is certainly not the whole grain story. Many other grains are readily available that are excellent both for cereals and breads.

All whole grains and whole-grain flours should be stored in the refrigerator. Since all bugs are born nutrition-oriented, they will always attack the whole grains first.

EASY NO-KNEAD BREAD

½ cup skim milk
2 tablespoons corn-oil margarine
1 tablespoon sugar
½ teaspoon salt
½ cup water
1 envelope active dry yeast (check date on package before
    using)
2 large egg whites
1½ cups whole-wheat flour
1½ cups unbleached all-purpose flour

1. Scald the milk (warm over medium heat until bubbles form around the edges of the saucepan). Remove from the heat and add the margarine, sugar, and salt. Stir until the margarine melts. Add the water and mix well. Add the yeast and mix well. Set aside.

2. Lightly beat the egg whites in a large mixing bowl. Add the milk mixture and mix well. Add the flours, one cup at a time, and mix until well blended and the dough forms a ball. Place the ball of dough in a large bowl which has been sprayed with a nonstick vegetable coating. Cover with a clean, damp towel and allow to rise in a warm place until doubled in bulk, about 1 hour.

3. Leaving it in the bowl, lightly flour (I use oat bran instead of flour because it makes a more attractive loaf of bread) the dough ball so that your hands won't stick to it, punch it down, and form into a loaf-shaped roll. Place the dough in a 9-by-5-inch loaf pan which has been sprayed with nonstick vegetable coating and bake in a preheated 350°F oven until golden brown and the loaf sounds hollow when lightly thumped with your finger, about 55 minutes.

MAKES 16 SERVINGS

Each serving contains approximately:
Calories / 100   Cholesterol / Negligible
Fat / 2g   Sodium / 100mg

PUMPKIN BREAD

I revised this recipe for my fellow King Features Syndicate columnist, Heloise. She then ran it in her famous "Hints from Heloise" column for all of her readers to enjoy.

1⅔ cups unbleached all-purpose flour
¾ cup sugar
1 teaspoon baking soda
1½ teaspoons ground cinnamon
¼ teaspoon salt
¼ cup chopped pecans
½ cup liquid egg substitute or 1 large egg and 2 large egg whites, beaten together
¼ cup canola oil
¼ cup frozen unsweetened apple juice concentrate, thawed
1 teaspoon vanilla extract
1 cup canned pumpkin (½ of a 16-ounce can)

1. Combine the flour, sugar, baking soda, cinnamon, salt, and pecans in a large bowl. Mix well.

2. In a separate bowl, combine the remaining ingredients, using a wire whisk to mix well. Add the liquid ingredients to the dry ingredients and mix just until moistened.

3. Pour the batter into a 9-by-5-by-3-inch loaf pan that has been sprayed with nonstick vegetable coating. Bake in a preheated 350°F oven until a knife inserted in the center comes out clean, about 70 to 75 minutes.

MAKES 16 SERVINGS

Each serving contains approximately:
Calories / 140   Cholesterol / 1mg
Fat / 5g   Sodium / 100mg

ZUCCHINI BREAD

1½ cups unbleached all-purpose flour
1½ cups whole-wheat flour
1 tablespoon ground cinnamon
½ teaspoon salt
1 teaspoon baking soda
1 teaspoon baking powder
¾ cup liquid egg substitute
½ cup sugar
½ firmly packed brown sugar
½ cup canola oil
⅔ cup buttermilk
2 teaspoons vanilla extract
½ pound zucchini, grated (2 cups)

1. Preheat the oven to 350°F. Combine the flours, cinnamon, salt, baking soda, and baking powder in a large bowl. In a separate bowl, combine the egg substitute, sugars, oil, buttermilk, and vanilla.

2. Add the liquid to the dry ingredients and mix just until moistened. Stir in the grated zucchini. Pour into two 8-by-4-by-2½-inch loaf pans sprayed with nonstick vegetable coating. Bake until golden brown and a knife inserted in the center comes out clean, about 50 to 60 minutes. Remove to a wire rack to cool slightly before slicing.

MAKES 2 LOAVES; 12 SERVINGS PER LOAF

Each serving contains approximately:
Calories / 126   Cholesterol / Negligible
Fat / 4g   Sodium / 135mg

STRAWBERRY BREAD

½ cup chopped walnuts, toasted in a 350°F oven until
   golden brown, 8 to 10 minutes
1 cup plus 1 tablespoon sugar
3 cups whole fresh strawberries or 3 cups frozen, thawed and
   drained
1 cup liquid egg substitute
½ cup canola oil
½ cup buttermilk
¼ cup firmly packed brown sugar
2 teaspoons vanilla extract
2 teaspoons ground cinnamon
3 cups unbleached all-purpose flour
1 teaspoon baking soda
½ teaspoon salt

1. In a medium-size bowl, sprinkle 1 tablespoon of the sugar over the strawberries. Gently mash to start the juices flowing, then let stand at room temperature 1 hour.

2. Using an electric mixer, blend the egg substitute, oil, buttermilk, white and brown sugars, vanilla, and cinnamon in a large bowl. Add the strawberries and mix well with a spoon. Add the flour, baking soda, and salt. Blend well and add the nuts.

3. Pour into two 9-by-5-inch loaf pans generously sprayed with nonstick vegetable coating. Tap the pans on a flat surface to remove any bubbles, then bake in a preheated 350°F oven until the bread is no longer soggy, 55 to 60 minutes. Let stand in the pan for 10 to 15 minutes before slicing.

MAKES 2 LOAVES; 16 SERVINGS PER LOAF

Each serving contains approximately:
Calories / 130   Cholesterol / Negligible
      Fat / 5g   Sodium / 82mg

PEANUTY APPLESAUCE DATE BREAD

1 cup unsweetened applesauce
⅓ cup unhomogenized chunky peanut butter
⅓ cup plain nonfat yogurt
3 tablespoons honey
2 large egg whites
1 tablespoon corn oil
1½ cups whole-wheat flour
¾ cup rolled oats
¼ cup wheat germ
1 teaspoon ground cinnamon
1 teaspoon baking soda
¼ teaspoon salt
1 cup chopped dried or fresh dates
½ cup chopped dry-roasted peanuts

1. Preheat the oven to 350°F. Combine the applesauce, peanut butter, yogurt, honey, egg whites, and corn oil in a large bowl until well mixed.

2. In another bowl, combine the flour, oats, wheat germ, cinnamon, soda, and salt. Add the dry ingredients to the liquid ingredients. Stir in the chopped dates and all but 2 tablespoons of the peanuts and pour the batter into an 8½-by-4½-by-2½-inch loaf pan that has been sprayed with nonstick vegetable coating.

3. Sprinkle the top with the remaining peanuts and bake until a wooden toothpick or a knife inserted in the center comes out clean, about 70 minutes. Cool on a wire rack before slicing.

MAKES 16 SERVINGS

Each serving contains approximately:
Calories / 185   Cholesterol / Negligible
Fat / 7g   Sodium / 99mg

BANANA BREAD

3 tablespoons buttermilk
1 teaspoon baking soda
⅔ cup sugar
⅓ cup canola oil
2 very ripe bananas, mashed
3 large egg whites, lightly beaten
1 cup unbleached all-purpose flour
1 cup whole-wheat flour
¼ cup chopped walnuts, toasted in a 350°F oven until
   golden brown, 8 to 10 minutes

1. Spray an 8-by-4-by-2½-inch loaf pan with nonstick vegetable coating. Combine the buttermilk and soda in a small bowl. Set aside.

2. Cream the sugar and oil together in a large bowl. Add the bananas, then the flours alternately with the egg whites. Add the buttermilk mixture and stir just until mixed. Gently stir in the toasted walnuts.

3. Pour the mixture into the prepared loaf pan and bake in a preheated 350°F oven until a toothpick inserted in the center comes out clean, 45 to 50 minutes.

MAKES 20 SERVINGS

Each serving contains approximately:
Calories / 129   Cholesterol / Negligible
Fat / 5g   Sodium / 50mg

CHEESE AND ONION BREAD

2 tablespoons plus 1 teaspoon corn-oil margarine
1 medium onion, chopped (1½ cups)
2 large egg whites
½ cup light sour cream
⅛ teaspoon freshly ground black pepper
2 cups unbleached all-purpose flour
1 tablespoon baking powder
4 ounces reduced-fat Cheddar cheese, shredded (1 cup)
⅔ cup skim milk
3 tablespoons minced fresh parsley

1. Preheat the oven to 425°F. Melt 1 teaspoon of the margarine in a medium-size nonstick skillet over medium heat. Cook the onion, stirring, until soft, about 5 minutes, and let cool slightly. Add the egg whites, sour cream, and pepper, mix well, and set aside.

2. In a large mixing bowl, combine the flour and baking powder. Cut in the remaining margarine with a pastry cutter or fork until crumbly and fine. Stir in half of the shredded cheese, add the milk, and stir to make a soft dough.

3. Pat the dough into a 9-inch square pan sprayed with nonstick vegetable coating. Spread the sour cream mixture on top, then sprinkle with the remaining cheese and the parsley. Bake until golden brown and no longer soggy, about 25 minutes. Cut into squares and serve immediately.

MAKES 8 SERVINGS

Each serving contains approximately:
Calories / 200   Cholesterol / 18mg
Fat / 6g   Sodium / 338mg

SUNSHINE HARVEST BREAD

8 to 9 cups unbleached all-purpose flour
2 packages active dry yeast (check date on package before using)
¼ cup sugar
1 tablespoon salt
¾ cup wheat germ
1½ cups zucchini milk made by pureeing 1¼ pounds peeled zucchini in food processor or blender until smooth
¼ cup frozen unsweetened apple juice concentrate, thawed
¼ cup water
6 tablespoons (¾ stick) corn-oil margarine
1 cup liquid egg substitute

1. In a large mixer bowl, combine 3 cups of the flour, the yeast, sugar, salt, and wheat germ, mixing well. In a small saucepan, heat the zucchini milk, apple juice concentrate, water, and margarine until warm, between 120°F and 130°F. Add the liquid mixture and the egg substitute to the flour mixture. Blend at low speed, then beat 3 minutes at medium speed.

2. By hand, gradually stir in enough flour to make a firm dough. Knead on a floured surface until smooth and elastic, 5 to 8 minutes. Place in a bowl sprayed with nonstick vegetable coating, turning so the top gets coated. Cover with a clean, damp towel and let rise in warm place until doubled in bulk, about 1½ hours.

3. Punch the dough down, divide into three parts, and shape into three loaves. Place in 8-by-4-inch loaf pans sprayed with nonstick vegetable coating. Cover and let rise in a warm place until doubled, about 45 minutes. Bake in a preheated 375°F oven until golden brown, 25 to 30 minutes. Remove from pans and cool on a wire rack.

MAKES 3 LOAVES; 16 SERVINGS PER LOAF

Each serving contains approximately:
Calories / 108   Cholesterol / Negligible
Fat / 2g   Sodium / 178mg

ALMOND POPPYSEED BREAD

3 cups unbleached all-purpose flour
1⅓ cups sugar
1½ teaspoons baking powder
1½ teaspoons baking soda
1 tablespoon poppyseeds
⅔ cup canola oil
2 large eggs
1 cup buttermilk
⅔ cup frozen unsweetened apple juice concentrate, thawed
1 tablespoon vanilla extract
1 tablespoon almond extract
1 tablespoon butter extract (optional)
Glaze (recipe follows)

1. In a large bowl, combine the flour, sugar, baking powder, baking soda, and poppyseeds.

2. In another large bowl, combine the oil, eggs, buttermilk, apple juice concentrate, and extracts. Mix well.

3. Add the liquid ingredients to the dry ingredients and mix just until moistened.

4. Divide the dough into two 9-by-5-inch loaf pans that have been sprayed with nonstick vegetable coating. Bake in a preheated 350°F oven until a toothpick inserted in the center comes out clean and dry, about 50 minutes. Remove from the pans onto a wire rack and cool. Brush with glaze.

MAKES 2 LOAVES; 16 SERVINGS PER LOAF

Each glazed serving contains approximately:
Calories / 150   Cholesterol / 14mg
Fat / 5g   Sodium / 74mg

GLAZE

¼ *cup orange juice*
½ *cup sugar*
½ *teaspoon vanilla extract*
½ *teaspoon almond extract*
½ *teaspoon butter extract (optional)*

1. Combine all the ingredients in a small saucepan. Cook over low heat until the sugar is dissolved.

2. Bring to a boil over medium heat, reduce the heat to low, and simmer 5 minutes. Brush on the bread while still warm.

MAKES ABOUT ½ CUP

1 teaspoon contains approximately:
Calories / 14   Cholesterol / None
Fat / None   Sodium / Negligible

FLAVORFUL SPINACH CORN BREAD

1 cup yellow cornmeal
1 cup unbleached all-purpose flour
1 tablespoon baking powder
½ teaspoon salt
2 tablespoons sugar
2 tablespoons corn oil
1 large egg, beaten
1 cup skim milk
One 10-ounce package frozen chopped spinach, thawed and
  squeezed dry
1 small onion, chopped (1 cup)
1 cup low-fat cottage cheese

1. Preheat the oven to 350°F. Combine all the ingredients in a large bowl and mix well.

2. Pour the mixture into an 8-by-8-by-2-inch baking dish which has been sprayed with nonstick vegetable spray. Bake until brown on the outside and set in the middle, about 35 minutes.

MAKES 6 SERVINGS

Each serving contains approximately:
Calories / 294   Cholesterol / 48mg
Fat / 7g   Sodium / 635mg

SOUTHWESTERN CORN BREAD

2 tablespoons corn oil
½ cup finely chopped onion
One 4-ounce can chopped green chilies, drained (½ cup)
One 2-ounce jar pimentos, drained and diced (¼ cup)
1 cup yellow cornmeal
1 cup unbleached all-purpose flour
1 tablespoon baking powder
½ teaspoon salt
½ teaspoon ground cumin
½ teaspoon chili powder
2 ounces coarsely grated sharp Cheddar cheese (½ cup)
1 cup skim milk
1 large egg
1 cup cooked corn kernels (fresh, frozen, or canned, drained)

1. Preheat the oven to 400°F. Place 1 teaspoon of the oil in a skillet over medium heat. Add the onions, green chilies, and pimento, and cook, stirring, until tender, about 5 minutes. Do not brown. Set aside.

2. In a large bowl, combine the cornmeal, flour, baking powder, salt, cumin, and chili powder. Add the cheese and mix again.

3. In a separate bowl, combine the remaining ingredients with the onion mixture and mix well. Add this mixture to the cornmeal mixture, mixing just until blended. Do not overmix.

4. Pour the batter into an 8-inch-square pan which has been sprayed with a nonstick vegetable coating. Bake until lightly browned and a toothpick inserted in the center comes out clean, 25 to 30 minutes. Cool 5 to 10 minutes before cutting.

MAKES 9 SERVINGS

Each serving contains approximately:
Calories / 200   Cholesterol / 40mg
Fat / 6g   Sodium / 295mg

MORNING GLORY MUFFINS

2 large carrots, grated (2 cups)
½ medium apple, peeled and diced (½ cup)
½ cup raisins, soaked in hot water to cover for several
  minutes and drained
¼ cup walnuts, chopped and toasted in a 350°F oven until
  golden brown, 8 to 10 minutes
½ cup frozen pineapple juice concentrate, thawed
¼ cup firmly packed brown sugar
4 tablespoons (½ stick) corn-oil margarine, softened
½ cup liquid egg substitute
2 teaspoons vanilla extract
½ teaspoon coconut extract
1 cup unbleached all-purpose flour
½ cup oat bran
½ cup wheat bran
2 teaspoons baking powder
1 teaspoon ground cinnamon
¼ teaspoon salt

1. Preheat the oven to 350°F. In a large mixing bowl, combine the carrots, apple, raisins, and walnuts. Set aside.

2. In a medium-size mixing bowl, mix together the pineapple juice concentrate, brown sugar, margarine, egg substitute, and extracts. In another bowl, combine the flour, oat bran, wheat bran, baking powder, cinnamon, and salt. Add to the carrot mixture and mix well.

3. Pour the liquid ingredients into the carrot-flour mixture and stir just until moistened. Spoon the batter into muffin tins sprayed with nonstick vegetable coating. Bake until the muffins are golden brown and a toothpick inserted in the center comes out clean, about 25 to 30 minutes. Let cool in the pan for 10 minutes before removing to a wire rack to finish cooling.

MAKES 12 MUFFINS

Each muffin contains approximately:
Calories / 189   Cholesterol / Negligible
Fat / 6g   Sodium / 152mg

HOLIDAY MUFFINS

2 cups unbleached all-purpose flour
¼ cup sugar
1 tablespoon baking powder
½ teaspoon baking soda
¼ teaspoon salt
¾ teaspoon freshly grated nutmeg
1 cup buttermilk
2 tablespoons water
2 tablespoons corn-oil margarine, melted
3 large egg whites
2 tablespoons frozen unsweetened apple juice concentrate, thawed
1½ teaspoons vanilla extract

1. Preheat the oven to 400°F. Combine the flour, sugar, baking powder, baking soda, salt, and nutmeg in a large bowl. In another bowl, combine the buttermilk, water, margarine, egg whites, apple juice concentrate, and vanilla.

2. Add the liquid to the dry ingredients and stir only until just moistened. Pour into twelve muffin cups sprayed with nonstick vegetable coating. Bake until a golden color and a toothpick inserted in the center comes out clean, about 20 minutes. Allow to cool in the pan for 10 minutes before removing to a wire rack to finish cooling.

MAKES 12 MUFFINS

Each muffin contains approximately:
Calories / 126   Cholesterol / 1mg
Fat / 2g   Sodium / 312mg

SMALL STREUSEL COFFEE CAKE

CAKE

¼ pound (1 stick) corn-oil margarine
1 cup sugar
4 large egg whites, lightly beaten
2 cups nonfat plain yogurt
1 tablespoon vanilla extract
2 teaspoons baking powder
2 teaspoons baking soda
3 cups unbleached all-purpose flour

STREUSEL

⅓ cup firmly packed brown sugar
2 tablespoons sugar
1 tablespoon corn-oil margarine, at room temperature
2 teaspoons cinnamon

1. Preheat the oven to 350°F. To make the cake, cream together the margarine and sugar in a large bowl. Add the egg whites, yogurt, and vanilla and mix well.

2. In a separate bowl, combine the baking powder, soda, and flour. Add to the liquid ingredients and mix well.

3. Combine all the streusel ingredients and mix well. Spray a 9-inch tube or bundt pan with nonstick vegetable coating. Pour half the batter into the pan, sprinkle with half the streusel, then add the remaining batter and sprinkle with the remaining streusel. Draw a knife through the batter to marble the cake.

4. Bake until golden, about 70 minutes. Cool on a rack for 5 minutes, then remove the cake from the pan.

MAKES 8 SERVINGS

Each serving contains approximately:
Calories / 467   Cholesterol / 1mg
Fat / 13g   Sodium / 618mg

PEACH KUCHEN

1 cup unbleached all-purpose flour
¼ teaspoon baking powder
¼ teaspoon salt
1½ teaspoons ground cinnamon
½ cup firmly packed brown sugar
4 tablespoons (½ stick) corn-oil margarine
12 canned or fresh peach halves or two 16-ounce cans juice-
    or water-packed peach halves, drained
¼ cup liquid egg substitute
1 cup canned evaporated skimmed milk
½ teaspoon vanilla extract

1. Preheat the oven to 400°F. Sift together the flour, baking powder, salt, ½ teaspoon of the cinnamon, and 1 tablespoon of the brown sugar. Cut in the margarine with 2 knives or a pastry blender until the mixture looks like cornmeal.

2. Pile the mixture into an 8-inch-square pan sprayed with nonstick vegetable coating and pat an even layer over the bottom and halfway up the sides of the pan. Place the peaches on top of the pastry. Combine the remaining brown sugar with the remaining cinnamon and sprinkle over the peaches. Bake for 15 minutes.

3. Combine the egg substitute, evaporated milk, and vanilla and pour over the baked mixture. Bake until the top is set, about 30 minutes longer.

MAKES 9 SERVINGS

Each serving contains approximately:
Calories / 192   Cholesterol / 1mg
Fat / 6g   Sodium / 199mg

SOUR CREAM COFFEE CAKE

4 tablespoons (½ stick) corn-oil margarine
¾ cup sugar
½ cup liquid egg substitute
1 cup light sour cream
1 teaspoon baking soda
1 teaspoon vanilla extract
1½ cups unbleached all-purpose flour
1½ teaspoons baking powder
½ cup walnuts, chopped and toasted in a 350°F oven until
golden brown, 8 to 10 minutes
2 teaspoons ground cinnamon

1. Preheat the oven to 350°F. Cream the margarine and ½ cup of the sugar together in a medium-size bowl until fluffy, add the egg substitute, and stir until combined.

2. In a small bowl, combine the sour cream and baking soda, then stir into the first mixture. Stir in the vanilla, then add the flour and baking powder and mix well.

3. Combine the toasted walnuts, the remaining sugar, and the cinnamon. Stir half of it into the batter, then pour the batter into a 9-inch-square pan. Sprinkle the remaining nut mixture over the top. Bake until a golden brown, about 50 minutes.

MAKES 9 SERVINGS

Each serving contains approximately:
Calories / 276   Cholesterol / 11mg
Fat / 13g   Sodium / 199mg

COFFEE RHUBARB CAKE

⅓ *cup corn-oil margarine*
1¼ *cups sugar*
2 *large egg whites*
1 *cup buttermilk*
1½ *teaspoons vanilla extract*
1 *teaspoon baking soda*
½ *cup hot coffee*
2 *cups unbleached all-purpose flour*
¼ *teaspoon salt*
1½ *large stalks rhubarb (8 ounces), leaves removed and diced*
   (2 cups)
1 *teaspoon ground cinnamon*

1. Preheat the oven to 350°F. Using a wooden spoon, cream the margarine and 1 cup plus 2 tablespoons of the sugar together in a large bowl. Add the egg whites, buttermilk, and vanilla and mix well. Dissolve the baking soda in 2 tablespoons of the hot coffee, then add it to the creamed mixture.

2. Combine the flour and salt and stir into the creamed mixture. Fold in the diced rhubarb and pour the batter into a 9-by-13-inch baking pan sprayed with nonstick vegetable coating. Combine the remaining sugar with the cinnamon and sprinkle over the batter.

3. Bake until the center of the cake springs back when pressed gently, about 35 to 40 minutes. Remove from the oven and brush the top of the hot cake with the remaining hot coffee.

MAKES 15 SERVINGS

Each serving contains approximately:
Calories / 173   Cholesterol / 1mg
Fat / 4g   Sodium / 175mg

LIGHT PANCAKES

2 large egg whites, beaten
¼ cup frozen unsweetened apple juice concentrate, thawed
1 teaspoon sugar
2 teaspoons vanilla extract
3 tablespoons unbleached all-purpose flour
2½ tablespoons instant nonfat dry milk
1 teaspoon baking powder

Mix all ingredients together in a small bowl until well combined. (A blender is ideal for this recipe.) Spray a frying pan with nonstick vegetable coating and let get hot over medium heat. For each pancake, spoon 2 to 3 tablespoons batter into the pan and cook until bubbles appear in the pancakes. Turn and brown the other side.

MAKES ABOUT 5 PANCAKES

Each pancake contains approximately:
Calories / 60   Cholesterol / Negligible
Fat / Negligible   Sodium / 169mg

IRISH BOXTY PANCAKES

¼ cup whole-wheat flour
¼ teaspoon baking powder
¼ teaspoon salt
One 8-ounce potato, peeled and grated
1 large egg white, lightly beaten
¼ cup skim milk
Oil, for wiping skillet

1. Combine the flour, baking powder, and salt and mix well. Add all remaining ingredients and again mix well.

2. Lightly oil and warm a heavy skillet over medium heat. To cook, for each pancake spoon a scant ¼ cup of the batter into the hot skillet and cook until golden brown, 3 to 4 minutes on each side.

MAKES 6 PANCAKES

Each pancake contains approximately:
Calories / 53   Cholesterol / Negligible
Fat / Negligible   Sodium / 143mg

DUTCH BABIES
(PANNEKOEKEN)

This recipe is a whole lot lighter than my Dutch grandmother's version of pannekoeken. However, I enjoy my Dutch Babies more often and with less guilt than her version would allow.

3 tablespoons corn-oil margarine
1 large egg plus 4 large egg whites
¾ cup skim milk
¾ cup whole-wheat flour

1. Preheat the oven to 425°F. Place the margarine in a small ovenproof pan or casserole. Place the pan in the oven to melt the margarine.

2. Combine the egg and egg whites in a blender and process on high speed for 30 seconds. With the motor running, slowly add the milk and then slowly add the flour. Blend for 30 seconds more.

3. Remove the pan from the oven and pour in the batter. Bake until puffy and a golden brown, 20 to 25 minutes. Cut into four wedges and serve immediately. (Don't be alarmed when the center falls—this is normal!)

MAKES 4 SERVINGS

Each serving contains approximately:
Calories / 203   Cholesterol / 54mg
Fat / 11g   Sodium / 207mg

BAKED FRENCH TOAST

I revised this recipe for a reader about a year ago. Now it is the way I always make French toast because it's so easy and so delicious.

10 slices whole-wheat bread
One 12-ounce can evaporated skimmed milk (1½ cups)
2 large eggs plus 4 large egg whites or 1 cup liquid egg substitute
⅓ cup firmly packed dark brown sugar
1 teaspoon vanilla extract
½ teaspoon ground cinnamon

1. Lightly spray a 9-by-13-by-2-inch dish with a nonstick vegetable coating. Arrange the bread slices in the dish (it will be a tight fit).

2. Combine all remaining ingredients and mix well with a wire whisk or egg beater. Pour the mixture evenly over the bread. Cover tightly and refrigerate several hours or overnight.

3. To bake, preheat the oven to 350°F. Remove the dish from the refrigerator and spray the bread lightly with nonstick vegetable coating. Bake until lightly browned, 30 to 35 minutes.

MAKES 5 SERVINGS

Each serving contains approximately:
Calories / 272   Cholesterol / 90mg
Fat / 4g   Sodium / 402mg

SOUTHWESTERN CORN CHIPS

This dough dries out very quickly, so don't make it until you are ready to make the chips. Keep the unused portions of dough covered with a damp towel while the chips are baking.

½ cup water
4 teaspoons corn-oil margarine
1 teaspoon chili powder
½ teaspoon garlic powder
¼ teaspoon ground cumin
⅛ teaspoon salt
⅔ cup yellow cornmeal

1. Preheat the oven to 375°F. Combine all the ingredients except the cornmeal in a saucepan and bring to a boil over medium heat. Remove from the heat and stir in the cornmeal, mixing well.

2. Divide the dough into thirty-six portions using about 1 teaspoon of dough for each portion. Roll each portion into a ball about ¾ inch in diameter. Lightly spray two baking sheets with nonstick vegetable coating. Space the dough balls on the baking sheets about 4 inches apart and cover them with a sheet of waxed paper.

3. Flatten each ball with a smooth-bottomed glass until very thin and 2 to 3 inches in diameter. Remove the waxed paper and bake immediately until golden brown and crisp, about 10 to 12 minutes. Cool on a rack and then store in an airtight container.

MAKES 36 CHIPS

Each chip contains approximately:
Calories / 14   Cholesterol / None
Fat / Negligible   Sodium / 14mg

BULGARIAN SPINACH DUMPLINGS

6 ounces day-old bread or rolls (about 6 slices bread)
1½ cups skim milk
2 tablespoons corn-oil margarine
1½ tablespoons unbleached all-purpose flour
1 pound fresh spinach, washed and chopped, or one 10-ounce
  package frozen chopped spinach, thawed and liquid
  squeezed out
¼ teaspoon salt
⅛ teaspoon freshly ground black pepper
¼ cup soft bread crumbs, toasted in a 350°F oven until
  golden, 5 to 10 minutes
2 ounces grated hard cheese such as Gruyère or Cheddar
  (½ cup)

1. Crumble the bread into a medium-size bowl. Add ½ cup
of the milk and allow to soak until soggy. Meanwhile, melt 1
tablespoon of the margarine in a heavy skillet over medium heat.
Stir in the flour and cook, stirring, for 1 minute; do not brown.
Add the remaining milk and bring to a boil, stirring constantly.
Reduce the heat to low and simmer until thick, stirring occasionally
to avoid scorching.

2. While the sauce is simmering, squeeze the excess milk
out of the bread and chop the spinach. Mix the thickened sauce
with the bread and spinach. Add the salt and pepper and mix well
and put the dough aside to rest 5 to 10 minutes.

3. Bring 4 quarts of water to a boil over high heat in a large
saucepan, then reduce the heat to a gentle boil. Scoop out balls
about 1½ inches in diameter and drop them into the water, 6 to
8 dumplings at a time. (The water should not be allowed to stop
boiling or the dumplings will be heavy.) If the dumplings collapse
in the water, add a little more soaked bread to the dough. If the
dumpling is too heavy and hard, add a little more milk to the
dough.

4. Poach the dumplings 5 to 6 minutes, then pass them through a bowl of cold water to prevent them from sticking to one another. Melt the remaining margarine in a skillet over low heat. Turn the dumplings briefly in the margarine as they come out of the cold water and place them on a plate and keep warm. When all the dumplings are cooked, combine the toasted bread crumbs with the grated cheese and scatter evenly over the dumplings.

MAKES 4 SERVINGS

Each serving contains approximately:
Calories / 315   Cholesterol / 18mg
Fat / 13g   Sodium / 729mg

JONES SCONES

1 cup sifted unbleached all-purpose flour
1 cup sifted whole-wheat pastry flour
1 teaspoon cream of tartar
1 teaspoon baking soda
1 tablespoon sugar
¾ cup buttermilk

1. Preheat the oven to 450°F. Sift together the flours, cream of tartar, baking soda, and sugar in a medium-size bowl. Slowly add the buttermilk to the flour mixture and mix to make a soft dough.

2. Divide the dough in half. Pat each portion out on a lightly floured board into a circle ¾ inch thick. Cut each circle into six wedges and place on an ungreased baking sheet. Bake until golden, about 10 to 12 minutes.

MAKES 12 SCONES

Each scone contains approximately:
Calories / 80   Cholesterol / Negligible
Fat / Negligible   Sodium / 85mg

NEW YORKSHIRE PUDDING

1 cup unbleached all-purpose flour
¼ teaspoon salt
½ cup skim milk
4 egg whites, beaten until frothy
½ cup water
2 tablespoons corn-oil margarine, at room temperature

1. Combine the flour and salt in a medium-size bowl. Make a well in the center and stir in the milk, then beat in the beaten egg whites and add the water and 1 tablespoon of the melted margarine. Beat by hand until smooth and large bubbles rise to the surface. Set aside for 1 hour.

2. Preheat the oven to 400°F. Place the remaining tablespoon of margarine into a hot 9-by-13-inch glass baking dish. Beat the batter again and pour into the baking dish. Bake for 20 minutes, reduce the heat to 350°F and bake until set, 10 to 15 minutes longer. Serve immediately.

MAKES 12 SERVINGS

Each serving contains approximately:
Calories / 57   Cholesterol / Negligible
Fat / 2g   Sodium / 97mg

DESSERTS

Fruit is the ideal dessert because it is naturally sweet and doesn't contain the fat found in most man-made sweets. It contains no cholesterol, is very low in sodium, and is packed with vitamins and fiber.

Even though everyone's favorite fruits may not be the same, I don't know of anyone who just plain doesn't like fruit. Due to both popular demand and modern refrigerated transportation, there is an incredible variety of fresh fruit available all over the country during most of the year. Vine- and tree-ripened fruits are always both sweeter and more flavorful, but they are not always available.

When you buy fruit that is not quite ripe, allow it to ripen at room temperature before refrigerating it. Refrigerate ripe fruit to prevent spoilage. Don't peel or slice fresh fruits until you are ready to serve them or they will lose some of their vitamin content, dry out, and some, such as apples, will turn brown. To prevent apples from discoloring, brush them with citrus juice immediately after slicing them.

Fresh fruit provides the optimum amount of vitamins, and there are many ways to add variety in serving them. You can combine several types of fruit; puree fruits to serve on other fruits as sauces; marinate in fruit juices, wines, or liqueurs; or combine fresh fruits with cooked or canned and dried fruits to create what the French call a composed compote. Fresh fruits also make wonderful accompaniments and sauces for all other types of desserts, such as custards, puddings, cakes, and pies.

Without destroying too many of the vitamins in fruit and still creating very healthy desserts, it is possible to steam, poach, bake, or broil fruit. You can also freeze fruit for sorbets, sherbets, and ice cream.

When poaching peaches, plums, apricots, or cherries, remove the pits before cooking. An interesting aside about these fruits is that the nutlike kernel in the center of the pits is potentially poisonous. I was horrified to learn this because as a child I used to open peach pits and eat the almond-flavored "nut" in the center. Fortunately I never had too many of them at one time because supposedly eight to ten of them, if chewed, can release enough hydrogen cyanide to kill you!

When fresh fruits are not available, there is a wide selection of canned fruits packed in water or natural juices without sugar added. Not only are they better for you, they also taste better than the insipidly sweet fruit packed in heavy syrup.

Dried fruits make wonderful sweet snacks, which can be eaten like cookies or candy. They also make delicious compotes and sauces when cooked. Their high caloric content can be understood easily when you realize that it takes almost six pounds of a fresh fruit to yield one pound of dried fruit. Raisins or currants have more moisture and flavor if you plump them up first by presoaking them for 15 minutes before adding them to a mixture. When adding them to baked goods, either soak them in water and drain them, or soak them in one of the liquids you are using in the recipe.

LIGHTER POUND CAKE

2¼ cups unbleached all-purpose flour
¾ teaspoon baking powder
¼ teaspoon baking soda
¼ teaspoon salt
⅛ teaspoon ground mace (optional)
½ cup corn-oil margarine
1 cup sugar
3 large egg whites
1½ teaspoons vanilla extract
¾ cup buttermilk

1. Preheat the oven to 350°F. In a medium-size mixing bowl, combine the flour, baking powder, baking soda, salt, and mace. Mix well and set aside.

2. In a separate large mixing bowl, cream together the margarine and sugar until smooth. Add the egg whites and vanilla and blend until satin smooth. Alternately add half the flour mixture and half the buttermilk, blending well after each addition. Repeat with the remaining flour and buttermilk.

3. Spoon the batter into a standard 8½-by-4½-inch loaf pan which has been sprayed with a nonstick vegetable coating. Bake for 1 hour. Remove from the oven and cool on a rack.

MAKES 16 SERVINGS

Each serving contains approximately:
Calories / 169   Cholesterol / Negligible
Fat / 6g   Sodium / 181mg

LIGHT LAZY DAISY CAKE

CAKE

1 cup old-fashioned oatmeal
1¼ cups boiling water
½ cup liquid egg substitute
2 tablespoons canola oil
½ cup sugar
¼ cup firmly packed dark brown sugar
6 tablespoons frozen unsweetened apple juice concentrate,
    thawed
1⅓ cups unbleached all-purpose flour
1 teaspoon baking soda
1 teaspoon ground cinnamon
¼ teaspoon salt

TOPPING

½ cup firmly packed dark brown sugar
¼ cup chopped walnuts
2 tablespoons corn-oil margarine, melted
3 tablespoons skim milk
½ teaspoon vanilla extract
½ teaspoon coconut extract

1. Preheat the oven to 350°F. Put the oats in a large bowl and cover with the boiling water. Let stand 10 minutes. Add all the other cake ingredients and mix well. Pour into a 9-by-13-inch baking pan that has been sprayed with nonstick vegetable coating and bake until a knife inserted in the center comes out clean, about 35 minutes.

2. Combine the topping ingredients and spread over the hot cake. Place under the broiler until bubbly, 2 to 3 minutes. Watch carefully to avoid scorching.

MAKES 12 SERVINGS

Each serving contains approximately:
Calories / 230   Cholesterol / Negligible
Fat / 7g   Sodium / 159mg

SOCK-IT-TO-ME-LIGHTLY CAKE

¼ *cup firmly packed brown sugar*
1½ *teaspoons ground cinnamon*
2¼ *cups unbleached all-purpose flour*
2 *teaspoons baking powder*
½ *teaspoon baking soda*
¾ *cup sugar*
2 *large eggs, beaten*
2 *large egg whites*
½ *cup canola oil*
1 *cup plain nonfat yogurt*
1 *teaspoon vanilla extract*
¼ *teaspoon coconut extract*
¼ *cup pecans, chopped*

1. Preheat the oven to 350°F. In a small bowl, combine the brown sugar and cinnamon. Set aside.

2. In a large bowl, mix together the flour, baking powder, baking soda, and sugar. Stir in the beaten eggs, egg whites, oil, yogurt, and extracts. Add the chopped pecans.

3. Pour half of the batter into a 10-inch bundt pan sprayed with nonstick vegetable coating. Sprinkle with the brown sugar-and-cinnamon mixture and pour the remaining batter on top. Bake until a toothpick inserted in the cake comes out clean, about 40 minutes.

MAKES 12 SERVINGS

Each serving contains approximately:
Calories / 290   Cholesterol / 46mg
Fat / 14g   Sodium / 148mg

BANANA PINEAPPLE CAKE

3 cups unbleached all-purpose flour
½ cup sugar
2 teaspoons baking powder
1 teaspoon baking soda
½ teaspoon salt
¾ cup liquid egg substitute
½ cup canola oil
½ cup plain nonfat yogurt
2 teaspoons vanilla extract
2 cups mashed ripe bananas (1 pound, or 4 small)
One 8-ounce can crushed pineapple in its own juice
1 tablespoon confectioners' sugar

1. Preheat the oven to 350°F. In a large bowl, thoroughly stir together the flour, sugar, baking powder, baking soda, and salt.

2. In a separate bowl, combine the egg substitute, oil, yogurt, vanilla, bananas, and undrained pineapple. Make a well in the center of the dry ingredients and add the liquid ingredients all at once, stirring until moistened.

3. Pour the batter into a 10-inch fluted tube pan sprayed with nonstick vegetable coating. Bake until a toothpick inserted in the cake comes out clean, 65 to 70 minutes. Cool in the pan 15 minutes, then remove from the pan and cool on a wire rack. Sift the confectioners' sugar over the top.

MAKES 16 SERVINGS

Each serving contains approximately:
Calories / 212   Cholesterol / Negligible
Fat / 8g   Sodium / 205mg

CHRISTMAS CAROL CAKE

½ cup canola oil
¾ cup frozen unsweetened apple juice concentrate, thawed
½ cup sugar
2 teaspoons vanilla extract
1 large egg
3 large egg whites
1 cup unbleached all-purpose flour
1 cup whole-wheat flour
1½ teaspoons ground cinnamon
1 teaspoon baking soda
3 apples, peeled, cored, and well diced
½ cup chopped walnuts, toasted in a 350°F oven until
    golden brown, 8 to 10 minutes
¾ cup raisins

1. Preheat the oven to 325°F. Generously spray a 10-inch bundt pan with nonstick vegetable coating. In a large bowl, combine the oil, apple juice concentrate, sugar, and vanilla. In a small bowl, beat together the egg and egg whites until well mixed. Combine the flours, cinnamon, and baking soda and add to the large bowl alternately with the egg mixture. Stir until all the ingredients are well combined.

2. Add the diced apples, toasted walnuts, and raisins. Bake until a toothpick inserted in the center comes out clean, about 70 minutes. Cool for 45 minutes, then invert on a platter. Enjoy plain or glazed (recipe follows).

MAKES 16 SERVINGS

Each (unglazed) serving contains approximately:
Calories / 210   Cholesterol / 13mg
Fat / 10g   Sodium / 66mg

GLAZE

1 cup sugar
½ teaspoon baking soda
½ cup buttermilk
¼ pound (1 stick) corn-oil margarine
1 tablespoon light corn syrup
1 teaspoon vanilla extract

Combine all the ingredients except the vanilla in a small saucepan and bring to a boil. Cook for 5 minutes, stirring occasionally. Remove from the heat and stir in the vanilla. Pour over the cake and decorate as desired.

MAKES ABOUT 1 CUP GLAZE

1 tablespoon contains approximately:
Calories / 107   Cholesterol / Negligible
Fat / 6g   Sodium / 102mg

CHOCOLATE SWIRL CHEESECAKE

½ cup graham-cracker crumbs
¾ cup plus 1 tablespoon sugar
1 tablespoon corn-oil margarine, melted
Two 8-ounce packages Neufchâtel cheese, at room
  temperature
½ cup light sour cream
1 teaspoon vanilla extract
¾ cup liquid egg substitute
¼ cup unsweetened cocoa powder

1. Preheat the oven to 325°F. In a small bowl, combine the graham-cracker crumbs with 1 tablespoon of the sugar and the melted margarine and mix well. Pat firmly into a 9-inch springform pan, covering the bottom and ½ inch up the sides. Set aside.

2. In a large bowl, beat the Neufchâtel cheese at high speed with an electric mixer until light and creamy. Gradually beat in ½ cup of the sugar. Mix in the sour cream and vanilla. Add the egg substitute, ¼ cup at a time, beating well after each addition.

3. Divide the batter in half. Beat the cocoa and the remaining sugar into the first half. Pour into the crumb-lined pan and cover with the plain batter. With a knife, swirl the plain batter with the chocolate batter to marbleize.

4. Bake the cheesecake until only a 2- to 3-inch circle in the center will shake, about 50 minutes. Cool at room temperature, then refrigerate until ready to serve.

MAKES 16 SERVINGS

Each serving contains approximately:
Calories / 152   Cholesterol / 25mg
Fat / 9g   Sodium / 168mg

"WINNING" LITTLE CHEESECAKES

CUPCAKES

3 large egg whites
8 ounces Neufchâtel cheese, at room temperature
8 ounces part-skim ricotta cheese
½ cup sugar
2 tablespoons canola oil
1 teaspoon vanilla extract
6 graham cracker squares, crushed (6 tablespoons)

FROSTING

½ cup light sour cream

¼ cup sugar
1 teaspoon vanilla extract

1. Preheat the oven to 350°F. In a medium-size bowl, beat the egg whites with a wire whisk or electric mixer until soft peaks form. Set aside. In a separate bowl, cream together the cheeses and sugar. Add the oil and vanilla and blend well. Fold the egg whites into the cheese mixture until completely combined.

2. Place one teaspoon of crushed graham cracker in each of eighteen paper muffin cups in muffin tins. Fill each cup to within ½ inch from the top and bake until golden, about 25 minutes. After removing the cakes from the oven, increase the temperature to 400°F.

3. Combine the frosting ingredients in a small ovenproof bowl. Bake 5 minutes, then remove from the oven and stir with a whisk to remove any lumps. After the cakes and frosting are cool, frost each cake with about 1 teaspoon frosting and refrigerate.

MAKES 18 CUPCAKES

Each cupcake contains approximately:
Calories / 191   Cholesterol / 70mg
Fat / 7g   Sodium / 100mg

CHOCOLATE TORTE

2 envelopes unflavored gelatin
½ cup cool water
1½ cups boiling water
¾ cup unsweetened cocoa powder
¼ cup corn-oil margarine, at room temperature
6 large egg whites
½ cup sugar
1 large angel-food cake (8 ounces), cut in small pieces

1. In a large bowl combine the gelatin and cool water and allow to soften 5 minutes. Add the boiling water and stir until the gelatin is completely dissolved. Add the cocoa powder and margarine and stir until the margarine has completely melted. Set aside to cool.

2. Beat the egg whites until foamy. Add the sugar, a little at a time, and beat until soft peaks form. Fold the egg whites into the cooled cocoa mixture until no streaks of white show. Fold in the angel-food cake and pour into a 9-inch springform pan which has been sprayed with nonstick vegetable coating. Refrigerate for several hours or overnight.

3. To serve, unmold onto a serving platter and slice into eight pieces.

MAKES 8 SERVINGS

Each serving contains approximately:
Calories / 210   Cholesterol / None
Fat / 7g   Sodium / 120mg

RHUBARB MERINGUE TORTE

CRUST

1½ cups unbleached all-purpose flour
¼ pound (1 stick) chilled corn-oil margarine
1 tablespoon sugar
¼ teaspoon salt

FILLING

1 pound fresh rhubarb, leaves removed and finely diced
  (3½ cups)

¼ *cup liquid egg substitute*
½ *cup canned evaporated skimmed milk*
½ *cup frozen unsweetened apple juice concentrate, thawed*
1 *teaspoon vanilla extract*
½ *cup sugar*
2 *tablespoons unbleached all-purpose flour*

MERINGUE

4 *large egg whites*
½ *cup sugar*
1 *teaspoon vanilla extract*

1. To make the crust, preheat the oven to 350°F. Spray a 9-by-13-inch baking dish with nonstick vegetable coating. Combine the crust ingredients in a medium-size bowl, then, using a fork or pastry blender, blend the ingredients until the dough mixture resembles small peas. Press the dough into the prepared pan and bake until golden brown, about 15 minutes. Remove from the oven and set aside.

2. For the filling, spread the diced rhubarb over the baked pie shell. In a medium-size saucepan, combine the remaining filling ingredients and mix well with a wire whisk while bringing the mixture to a boil over medium heat. Stir constantly until thickened. Pour over the rhubarb and bake until the rhubarb is fork tender, about 20 minutes.

3. While the rhubarb is baking, make the meringue. In a medium-size bowl, beat the egg whites until frothy. Add the sugar, a tablespoon at a time, beating just until stiff peaks form; don't allow them to become dry. Beat in the vanilla. Top the rhubarb with the meringue and bake until golden brown, about 10 minutes.

MAKES 12 SERVINGS

Each serving contains approximately:
Calories / 242   Cholesterol / Negligible
Fat / 8g   Sodium / 196mg

CHRISTMAS PUDDING

1 cup grated peeled Russet potato
1 cup grated scraped carrots
¼ pound (1 stick) corn-oil margarine, softened
1 cup unbleached all-purpose flour
⅔ cup fructose or 1 cup sugar
1 cup raisins
1 cup currants (optional)
1 cup mixed chopped candied citrus peel
½ teaspoon ground cinnamon
½ teaspoon ground cloves
½ teaspoon freshly grated nutmeg
¼ teaspoon salt
½ teaspoon vinegar
2 tablespoons low-fat milk
½ teaspoon baking soda
Fresh mint or holly for garnish (optional)

1. Combine all the ingredients except the vinegar, milk, and soda. Mix well.

2. Add the vinegar to the milk, then mix in the baking soda. Add to the other ingredients and mix well.

3. Cook over simmering water in the top of a double boiler which has been sprayed with nonstick vegetable coating until a knife inserted in the center comes out clean, about 3 hours. Add boiling water to the bottom of the double boiler as needed.

4. To serve, unmold the pudding onto a serving platter and let rest for 10 to 15 minutes before slicing. Garnish as desired with fresh mint sprigs or, for a more festive occasion, holly leaves.

MAKES 12 SERVINGS

Each serving contains approximately:
Calories / 265   Cholesterol / Negligible
Fat / 8g   Sodium / 190mg

DELIGHTFUL BREAD PUDDING

One 1-pound loaf Vienna or French bread, cut into 1½-inch
    cubes and left to dry overnight
2 large eggs
5 large egg whites
1 cup sugar
3½ cups low-fat milk
1½ cups canned evaporated skimmed milk
1 tablespoon vanilla extract
⅓ cup golden seedless raisins

CARAMEL SAUCE

2 tablespoons corn-oil margarine
¾ cup firmly packed dark brown sugar
¼ cup low-fat milk
1 tablespoon cornstarch
1 teaspoon vanilla extract

1. Preheat the oven to 325°F. Beat the whole eggs and the
egg whites together in a large bowl with a whisk or an electric
mixer until frothy. Blend in the sugar. Gradually beat in the low-
fat and evaporated milk, and the vanilla.

2. Combine the bread cubes and raisins in a large mixing
bowl. Pour the milk mixture over them and mix well.

3. Pour into a 13-by-9-inch baking pan that has been sprayed
with a nonstick vegetable coating. Bake until a knife inserted near
the center comes out clean, 60 to 70 minutes. (If bread begins to
brown excessively, cover lightly with aluminum foil.)

4. While the pudding is cooking, combine the margarine,
sugar, milk, and cornstarch in a small saucepan. Cook over medium
heat, stirring constantly with a wire whisk, until the mixture thickens and comes to a boil. Continue to boil 1 minute.

5. Remove from the heat and stir in the vanilla. To serve,
spoon the pudding, warm or cold, into champagne glasses and top
with the warm sauce.

MAKES 12 SERVINGS

Each serving contains approximately:
Calories / 355   Cholesterol / 55mg
Fat / 6g   Sodium / 367mg

ALMOND RICE PUDDING

1½ cups skim milk
1¾ cups water
¼ teaspoon salt
½ cup long-grain brown rice
1 envelope unflavored gelatin
1½ teaspoons vanilla extract
½ cup sugar
1½ cups very cold canned evaporated skimmed milk
½ cup chopped raw almonds, toasted in a 350°F oven until
  golden brown, 8 to 10 minutes

1. Combine the milk, 1½ cups water, and salt in a heavy saucepan and bring to a boil. Slowly add the rice, stirring constantly for 2 minutes. Reduce the heat to very low and cook, covered, for 1 hour, stirring occasionally.

2. Soften the gelatin in ¼ cup cold water and add to the hot rice mixture. Stir until completely dissolved. Add the vanilla and half of the sugar. Mix well and set aside to cool.

4. Place the evaporated milk in a cold mixing bowl and beat at high speed with an electric mixer or a wire whisk until soft peaks form. Slowly beat in the remaining sugar. Fold the whipped milk and toasted almonds into the cooled rice mixture and chill until firm, at least 3 hours. Serve with fresh fruit.

MAKES TWENTY ½-CUP SERVINGS

Each serving contains approximately:
Calories / 83   Cholesterol / 1mg
Fat / 2g   Sodium / 63mg

CARROT PUDDING

4 *tablespoons (½ stick) corn-oil margarine*
⅓ *cup firmly packed dark brown sugar*
½ *cup frozen unsweetened apple juice concentrate, thawed*
½ *cup liquid egg substitute*
1 *teaspoon baking soda*
2 *teaspoons baking powder*
1 *teaspoon ground cinnamon*
½ *teaspoon freshly grated nutmeg*
1½ *cups whole-wheat flour*
2 *tablespoons fresh lemon juice*
2 *teaspoons grated lemon peel*
½ *pound carrots, grated (2 cups)*

1. Preheat the oven to 350°F. Cream together the margarine and sugar in a large bowl. Add the apple juice concentrate and egg substitute and mix well.

2. In a separate bowl, combine the baking soda, baking powder, cinnamon, nutmeg, and flour. Add to the liquid ingredients and mix well.

3. Add the lemon juice, lemon peel, and carrots to the batter mixture and mix until well combined. Pour into a 9-inch round or square cake pan and bake until a knife inserted in the center comes out clean, about 1 hour.

MAKES 12 SERVINGS

Each serving contains approximately:
Calories / 145   Cholesterol / Negligible
Fat / 5g   Sodium / 227mg

PERSIMMON PUDDING CAKE

This cake is a sensational substitute for the higher-calorie holiday desserts such as plum pudding and fruit cake. I like to serve it with this brandy-flavored topping, which replaces the more traditional hard sauce made with butter and sugar.

⅔ cup sugar
⅓ cup canola oil
1 cup sifted unbleached all-purpose flour
¼ teaspoon salt
1 teaspoon ground cinnamon
¼ teaspoon freshly grated nutmeg
2 teaspoons baking soda
2 teaspoons warm water
2 very ripe persimmons (12 ounces), peeled, seeded, and finely diced (see Note below)
3 tablespoons brandy
1 teaspoon vanilla extract
½ cup liquid egg substitute
½ cup seedless raisins
½ cup chopped walnuts
Topping (recipe follows, optional)

1. Preheat the oven to 350°F. In a large bowl, stir together the sugar and oil. In a small bowl, sift together the flour, salt, cinnamon, and nutmeg and add to the sugar and oil. (The batter will be stiff and crumbly.) Dissolve the baking soda in the warm water and add it to the batter, mixing well.

2. Mix the persimmons, brandy, and vanilla together in a separate bowl, then add to the batter. Add the egg substitute, mixing thoroughly but lightly. Add the raisins and nuts and stir until mixed.

3. Pour the batter into a 9-by-5-by-3-inch loaf pan lined with aluminum foil and sprayed with nonstick vegetable coating. Bake until a toothpick inserted in the center comes out clean, about 45

minutes. Pull the pudding cake out of the pan by the foil and cool. Serve each slice with 1 tablespoon topping, if desired.

MAKES 16 SERVINGS

Each serving (with topping) contains approximately:
Calories / 210   Cholesterol / 5mg
Fat / 8g   Sodium / 175mg

TOPPING

1 cup part-skim ricotta cheese
3 tablespoons plain nonfat yogurt
3 tablespoons sugar
1 teaspoon vanilla extract
1 tablespoon brandy

Blend all the ingredients together in a food processor with a metal blade until satin smooth. Refrigerate in a tightly covered container.

MAKES 1 CUP

1 tablespoon contains approximately:
Calories / 35   Cholesterol / 5mg
Fat / 1g   Sodium / 22mg

NOTE: When ripe, persimmons should have a red-orange skin and flesh and should be plump and soft but not mushy. The skin should be smooth, glossy, and brightly colored. Persimmons that are not ripe can be ripened at room temperature and ripe fruit may be stored in the refrigerator for up to three days. Some persimmons may have a few seeds, which should be removed before using the flesh in baked goods, puddings, and other desserts.

RUM BRANDY APPLE CAKE

¾ cup frozen unsweetened apple juice concentrate, thawed
¾ cup sugar
½ cup liquid egg substitute
¼ cup canola oil
¼ cup plus ½ teaspoon rum
¼ cup brandy
1 teaspoon vanilla extract
1 cup unbleached all-purpose flour
1 cup whole-wheat flour
2 teaspoons ground cinnamon
2 teaspoons baking soda
½ teaspoon ground cloves
½ teaspoon freshly grated nutmeg
¼ cup raisins
½ cup chopped walnuts, toasted in a 350°F oven until
    golden brown, 8 to 10 minutes
4 cups peeled, cored, and sliced apples
⅓ cup fruit-only strawberry preserves

1. Preheat the oven to 350°F. In a large bowl, combine the apple juice concentrate, sugar, egg substitute, oil, ¼ cup of the rum, the brandy, and vanilla.

2. In a separate bowl, combine the flours, cinnamon, baking soda, cloves, nutmeg, raisins, and walnuts. Add the dry to the liquid ingredients and stir until just moistened. Add the apples and stir.

3. Pour the batter into a 10-inch bundt pan generously sprayed with nonstick vegetable coating and bake 1 hour. Remove from the oven and cool 10 minutes in the pan. Remove from the pan and cool on a wire rack. While the cake is cooling, melt the preserves over low heat, then add the remaining rum, mix well, and drizzle over the cake.

MAKES 16 SERVINGS

Each serving contains approximately:
Calories / 220   Cholesterol / Negligible
Fat / 6g   Sodium / 120mg

APPLE YOGURT CAKE

2¼ cups unbleached all-purpose flour
2 teaspoons baking powder
½ teaspoon baking soda
¾ cup sugar
2 large eggs, beaten
2 large egg whites
½ cup canola oil
1 cup plain nonfat yogurt
2½ cups cooking apples, cored and diced
½ cup chopped nuts
Apple Glaze (recipe follows, optional)

1. Preheat the oven to 350°F. In a large bowl, combine the flour, baking powder, baking soda, and sugar. Stir in the beaten eggs, egg whites, oil, and yogurt. Mix well. Add the apples and nuts.

2. Pour the batter into a 10-inch bundt pan generously sprayed with nonstick vegetable coating. Bake until a toothpick inserted in the cake comes out clean, about 40 minutes. Cool on a wire rack. Brush on the glaze, if desired.

MAKES 16 SERVINGS

Each serving (without glaze) contains approximately:
Calories / 213   Cholesterol / 34mg
Fat / 10g   Sodium / 110mg

APPLE GLAZE

2 tablespoons frozen unsweetened apple juice concentrate, thawed
¼ cup sugar

Combine the concentrate and sugar in a small saucepan. Cook over low heat until the sugar is dissolved. Bring the mixture to a boil, reduce the heat, and simmer for 5 minutes.

MAKES ABOUT ¼ CUP GLAZE

¾ teaspoon contains approximately:
Calories / 16   Cholesterol / None
Fat / Negligible   Sodium / 1mg

APPLE TART

PASTRY CRUST

1 cup unbleached all-purpose flour
Pinch of salt
1 tablespoon sugar
6 tablespoons (¾ stick) cold corn-oil margarine, cut into small pieces
3 tablespoons cold water

PASTRY CREAM

¾ cup plus 2 tablespoons skim milk
Pinch of salt
⅓ cup sugar
⅓ cup unbleached all-purpose flour
½ cup liquid egg substitute
1 tablespoon dark rum
1 teaspoon vanilla extract

TOPPING

*3 Golden Delicious apples, peeled, cored, and cut into thin
  slices*
¼ cup sugar
¼ cup liquid egg substitute
1 tablespoon corn-oil margarine, melted
¼ cup raw almonds, chopped

1. For the crust, place the flour, salt, sugar, and margarine
in a medium-size bowl and mix to a fine-crumbed texture. Gradually mix in the cold water. The dough should hold together but
not be sticky. Shape into a disk about 5 inches in diameter. Wrap
in plastic and refrigerate for at least 30 minutes.

2. In a medium-size saucepan, bring the milk and salt to a
boil. While the milk is heating, whisk the sugar, flour, and egg
substitute together in a bowl. Gradually add the hot milk while
continuing to mix with the whisk. Return the mixture to the saucepan and heat to boiling, stirring constantly. When two or three
bubbles appear, remove from heat. Stir in the rum and vanilla and
pour into a bowl to cool.

3. Preheat the oven to 450°F. On a floured board, roll the
chilled dough into a circle. Line a 9-inch tart or pie pan with the
dough, trim the edges even with the top of the pan, and prick
the bottom with a fork.

4. Spread the pastry cream over the crust and top with the
apple slices, starting with the outside edge and overlapping in
concentric circles. Bake for 10 minutes, then lower the oven temperature to 400°F and bake another 30 minutes.

5. For the topping, mix together the sugar, egg substitute,
and margarine. Pour over the apples, sprinkle with the almonds,
and bake until the tart is well browned, 10 to 15 minutes.

MAKES 8 SERVINGS

Each serving contains approximately:
Calories / 312   Cholesterol / 1mg
Fat / 14g   Sodium / 126mg

APPLE DUMPLINGS WITH BRANDY SAUCE

DUMPLINGS

2 cups unbleached all-purpose flour
¼ teaspoon salt
¼ pound (1 stick) corn-oil margarine, cut into pieces
⅔ cup plain nonfat yogurt
6 medium tart cooking apples, cored and peeled
⅓ cup sugar
⅓ cup chopped pecans
1 tablespoon corn-oil margarine, at room temperature
Skim milk for brushing

SAUCE

½ cup firmly packed brown sugar
1 tablespoon corn-oil margarine
½ cup canned evaporated skimmed milk
1 tablespoon brandy or 1 teaspoon brandy extract

1. Preheat the oven to 400°F. In a medium-size bowl stir together the flour and salt. Cut in the margarine with two knives or a pastry blender until the mixture forms coarse crumbs. With a fork stir in the yogurt until the mixture leaves the sides of the bowl and forms a ball.

2. On a lightly floured surface, roll the dough into a 19-by-12-inch rectangle and cut a 1-inch strip off the 19-inch end. Cut the remaining dough into six 6-inch squares. Place an apple in the center of each square. In a small bowl stir together the sugar, pecans, and softened margarine. Stuff 1½ tablespoons of this mixture into the center of each apple. Fold the dough up around the apple, sealing the seams well. Place seam-side down on a greased 15-by-10-by-1-inch jelly-roll pan or baking sheet. Brush the dough with milk and prick with a fork.

3. Cut leaf designs out of the remaining 1-inch strip of dough. Brush with milk and place on top of the wrapped apples.

Bake until the apples are fork tender, 35 to 50 minutes. If the crusts brown too quickly, cover with aluminum foil.

4. In a small saucepan, combine all the sauce ingredients. Cook over medium heat, stirring often, until the mixture comes to a full boil, 3 to 4 minutes. Serve the sauce over the warm apple dumplings.

MAKES SIX DUMPLINGS

Each dumpling contains approximately:
Calories / 574   Cholesterol / 1mg
Fat / 24g   Sodium / 370mg

DUTCH APPLE PIE

CRUST

2 tablespoons corn-oil margarine, at room temperature
10 graham-cracker squares, crushed into crumbs (²/₃ cup)

FILLING

5½ cups peeled, cored, and sliced Rome apples (4 large or 1½ pounds)
1 tablespoon fresh lemon juice
2 tablespoons frozen unsweetened apple juice concentrate, thawed
3 tablespoons whole-wheat flour
¾ teaspoon ground cinnamon
¼ teaspoon freshly grated nutmeg
½ teaspoon vanilla extract

TOPPING

½ cup whole-wheat flour
2 tablespoons firmly packed dark brown sugar
1 tablespoon corn-oil margarine

1. Preheat the oven to 375°F. Combine the margarine and cracker crumbs. Press firmly onto the bottom and sides of a 9-inch pie pan. Bake 5 minutes.

2. In a large bowl, mix all the filling ingredients together and place in the crust. It is easier to layer the slices instead of dumping them into the crust.

3. In a small bowl, mix the topping ingredients together with a fork until crumbly. Sprinkle evenly over the apple pie mixture. Bake on a baking sheet until the top is golden and the filling is bubbling, about 50 minutes. If the pie looks like it is drying out on top, cover with aluminum foil. Cool on a wire rack and serve at room temperature.

MAKES 6 SERVINGS

Each serving contains approximately:
Calories / 246   Cholesterol / None
Fat / 7g   Sodium / 146mg

ZUCCHINI "APPLE" PIE

FILLING

1½ pounds medium zucchini, peeled, halved lengthwise, and
    cut crosswise into thin slices (4 cups)
½ cup sugar
⅓ cup packed light brown sugar
¼ cup unbleached all-purpose flour
¼ cup buttermilk
1 tablespoon cider vinegar
1 tablespoon water
1 teaspoon fresh lemon juice

½ *teaspoon ground cinnamon*
½ *teaspoon freshly grated nutmeg*
1 *frozen 9-inch pie shell, baked according to package*
  instructions

CRUMB TOPPING

4 *tablespoons (½ stick) corn-oil margarine*
⅓ *cup firmly packed light brown sugar*
⅔ *cup unbleached all-purpose flour*

1. Put all the filling ingredients into a 2-quart microwave-safe bowl. Stir to mix. Microwave, uncovered, on high, stirring 3 times, until thickened, 8 to 11 minutes. Pour into the baked pie shell.

2. To make the topping, melt the margarine in a small microwave-safe bowl. Stir in the remaining topping ingredients until blended. Cover with a lid or vented plastic wrap and microwave on high, stirring twice, until bubbly, 1½ to 2½ minutes.

3. Spread the topping out on a piece of aluminum foil. When cool enough to handle, sprinkle evenly over the filled pie. Chill in the refrigerator at least 3 hours.

MAKES 8 SERVINGS

Each serving contains approximately:
Calories / 348   Cholesterol / Negligible
Fat / 14g   Sodium / 221mg

WINTER FRUIT DELIGHT

1 envelope unflavored gelatin
One 1-pound can water-packed apricot halves, ½ cup of its
  liquid reserved and fruit diced
4 ounces Neufchâtel cheese, at room temperature
1 cup light sour cream
¼ cup sugar
One 20-ounce can unsweetened crushed pineapple, drained
2 large navel oranges, peeled and diced

1. In a small saucepan, soften the gelatin in the reserved apricot liquid for 5 minutes, then place the pan over low heat and stir until the gelatin is completely dissolved. *Do not boil.* Set aside.

2. In a large bowl, blend togethger the cheese, sour cream, and sugar. Add the dissolved gelatin and mix well. Add the apricots, pineapple, and oranges and again mix well. Pour the mixture into an 8-inch-square baking dish, cover tightly with aluminum foil or plastic wrap, and refrigerate for several hours or overnight before serving. This dish can be frozen, but should be allowed to thaw for 1 hour before serving.

MAKES TWELVE ½-CUP SERVINGS

Each serving contains approximately:
Calories / 123   Cholesterol / 15mg
Fat / 5g   Sodium / 51mg

FANTASY LEMON MOUSSE

1 envelope unflavored gelatin
2 tablespoons cool water

¼ cup boiling water
2 large egg whites, at room temperature
½ cup instant nonfat dry milk
½ cup water
¼ cup sugar
3 tablespoons fresh lemon juice
1 tablespoon bitters (see Note below)
1 teaspoon finely grated lemon peel

1. In a small bowl, soften the gelatin in the cool water for 5 minutes. Add the boiling water and stir until the gelatin is dissolved. Set aside.

2. Combine the egg whites, dry milk, and ½ cup water in a large bowl. Beat rapidly with a whisk or an electric mixer until firm peaks form. Add the dissolved gelatin and continue beating until thoroughly mixed.

3. Mix together the sugar, lemon juice, bitters, and ½ teaspoon of the lemon peel. Fold into the egg-white mixture until the color is even and no streaks of white show.

4. Pour into a 1½-quart mold, a 10-inch mold, or individual ½-cup ramekins. Sprinkle with the remaining lemon peel and refrigerate until firm, about 4 to 6 hours, or overnight. Serve on individual dessert plates, in large goblets, or in ramekins.

MAKES TEN ½-CUP SERVINGS

Each serving contains approximately:
Calories / 40   Cholesterol / 1mg
Fat / Negligible   Sodium / 35mg

NOTE: Bitters is a liquid made from the distillation of aromatic herbs, barks, roots, and plants, and it can be found in some liquor stores to flavor cocktails, or in the sauce and spice section of your supermarket near the Worcestershire sauce.

STRAWBERRY MOUSSE

Henry Haller, executive chef at the White House for many years, told me that his Strawberry Mousse was the most frequently requested dessert by each of the five presidents for whom he worked. I'm sure my revision will be as popular with your family as it was with all of those First Families in Washington.

2 envelopes unflavored gelatin
¼ cup cool water
¼ cup boiling water
3 tablespoons Cointreau
One 16-ounce package frozen unsweetened strawberries (2 cups), thawed
Juice of 1 lemon
⅓ cup sugar
½ cup instant nonfat dry milk
½ cup water
2 large egg whites, at room temperature
Raspberry Sauce (recipe follows)
Fresh strawberries and mint leaves for garnish

1. In a small bowl, soften the gelatin for 5 minutes in the ¼ cup cool water. Add the boiling water and stir until the gelatin is dissolved. Add the Cointreau, mix well, and set aside.

2. In a blender, puree the strawberries. Add the lemon juice, sugar, and gelatin mixture. Mix well.

3. In a small bowl, combine the dry milk, ½ cup water, and egg whites. Beat with an electric mixer or wire whisk until stiff peaks form. Transfer to a large bowl and fold in the strawberry mixture, mixing just until blended.

4. Pour into a 9-inch bundt pan or 2-quart mold and refrigerate until firm, at least 4 hours, or overnight. To unmold, dip mold briefly in hot water and turn onto a serving plate. Drizzle the Raspberry Sauce over the top and garnish with fresh strawberries and mint leaves.

MAKES TEN ¾-CUP SERVINGS

Each serving contains approximately:
Calories / 104   Cholesterol / 1mg
Fat / Negligible   Sodium / 32mg

RASPBERRY SAUCE

One 12-ounce package unsweetened raspberries, thawed
1 tablespoon Cointreau
¼ cup sugar
Juice of ½ lemon

1. Process the raspberries in a blender until smooth. Pour through a strainer to remove the seeds.

2. Add the Cointreau, sugar, and lemon juice and mix well. Refrigerate, tightly covered, until needed. Mix well before using.

MAKES ¾ CUP

1 tablespoon contains approximately:
Calories / 35   Cholesterol / None
Fat / Negligible   Sodium / Negligible

COCOA BROWNIES

½ cup boiling water
½ cup unsweetened cocoa powder
1½ cups sugar
⅓ cup canola oil
1 teaspoon vanilla extract
4 large egg whites, at room temperature
1¼ cups unbleached all-purpose flour
1 teaspoon baking powder
¼ teaspoon salt

1. Preheat the oven to 350°F. In a large bowl, combine the boiling water and cocoa. Mix with a wire whisk until well blended and smooth.

2. Add the sugar, oil, vanilla, egg whites, flour, baking powder, and salt. Mix well with a wire whisk.

3. Pour into a 9-by-13-inch pan which has been sprayed with a nonstick vegetable coating. Bake for 25 minutes.

MAKES 32 BARS

Each bar contains approximately:
Calories / 83   Cholesterol / None
Fat / 3g   Sodium / 38mg

MOLASSES BROWNIES

These unusual brownies are wonderful for brown-bag lunches. I even like them for breakfast!

⅓ cup chopped walnuts, toasted in a 350°F oven until
*   golden brown, 8 to 10 minutes*
3 large egg whites
1 tablespoon canola oil
¼ cup molasses
2 teaspoons vanilla extract
½ cup wheat germ
½ cup oat bran
½ cup instant nonfat dry milk
½ teaspoon baking powder
⅛ teaspoon salt

1. Preheat the oven to 325°F. Combine the egg whites, oil, molasses, and vanilla in a small bowl and mix well.

2. In a medium-size bowl, combine the oat bran, dry milk,

baking powder, and salt, and mix well. Pour the liquid ingredients into the dry ingredients, add the nuts, and mix well.

3. Spray an 8-inch square baking pan with nonstick vegetable coating. Spoon the batter into the pan and spread evenly. Bake until golden brown, about 30 minutes. Remove from the oven and cool on a wire rack. Invert the pan on a cutting board to remove, then cut into pieces.

MAKES 16 BROWNIES OR 64 BITE-SIZE TREATS

Each brownie contains approximately:
Calories / 70   Cholesterol / Negligible
Fat / 3g   Sodium / 59mg

Each treat contains approximately:
Calories / 18   Cholesterol / Negligible
Fat / 1g   Sodium / 15mg

DATE GEMS

1 cup whole-wheat flour
1 teaspoon baking powder
1 teaspoon ground cinnamon
¼ cup corn-oil margarine, at room temperature
¼ cup liquid egg substitute
½ cup frozen unsweetened apple juice concentrate, thawed
½ cup chopped dried dates or apricots
½ cup raisins
⅓ cup walnuts, chopped and toasted in a 350°F oven until golden brown, 8 to 10 minutes
2 tablespoons sunflower seeds, toasted with the walnuts

Preheat the oven to 350°F. In a medium-size mixing bowl, combine the flour, baking powder, and cinnamon. Stir in all the remaining ingredients and mix well. Drop by rounded teaspoons-ful onto an ungreased baking sheet. Bake until golden brown, about 15 minutes.

MAKES 24 COOKIES

Each cookie contains approximately:
Calories / 80   Cholesterol / Negligible
Fat / 4g   Sodium / 60mg

CHERRY BRUNCH BARS

2 tablespoons cornstarch
⅓ cup water
One 16-ounce can tart water-packed cherries
1⅓ cups sugar
5 large egg whites
¼ pound (1 stick) corn-oil margarine
1 egg
½ cup buttermilk
1 teaspoon vanilla extract
3 cups unbleached all-purpose flour
1½ teaspoons baking powder
¼ teaspoon salt

1. Preheat the oven to 350°F. Dissolve the cornstarch in the water. Drain the liquid from cherries into a medium-size saucepan. Add ⅓ cup of the sugar and stir over low heat until the sugar is dissolved. Add the cherries and the cornstarch mixture and stir until thickened.

2. Vigorously beat the egg whites in a large bowl until stiff but not dry. Set aside. In another bowl, cream the margarine and the remaining sugar until light and fluffy. Gradually add the whole

egg and the buttermilk, then the vanilla. Combine the dry ingredients and add to the creamed mixture, mixing well. Fold in the beaten egg whites until well combined and no streaks of white remain.

3. Spread two thirds of the batter in the bottom of a jelly-roll pan sprayed with a nonstick vegetable coating. Spread with the cherry mixture and drop spoonfuls of the remaining batter on top. Bake until golden brown, about 30 minutes.

MAKES 15 SERVINGS

Each serving contains approximately:
Calories / 240   Cholesterol / 15mg
Fat / 7g   Sodium / 198mg

NECTARINE CRUNCH BARS

1 pound fresh nectarines or peaches, peeled, stoned, and diced (2 cups)
2 tablespoons sugar
2 tablespoons fresh lemon juice
2 tablespoons water
1½ teaspoons cornstarch
¼ teaspoon almond extract
1 cup unbleached all-purpose flour
1 cup old-fashioned oatmeal
½ cup wheat germ
¼ cup firmly packed brown sugar
½ teaspoon ground cinnamon
¼ teaspoon salt
¼ cup frozen unsweetened apple juice concentrate, thawed
¼ pound (1 stick) corn-oil margarine

1. Combine the nectarines, sugar, and lemon juice in a medium-size saucepan. Cook over medium heat, stirring constantly,

for 3 minutes. Combine the water and cornstarch, stirring until the cornstarch is dissolved, and add it to the nectarine mixture. Cook and stir until thickened. Remove from the heat and add the almond extract. Let cool.

2. Preheat the oven to 350°F. In a large bowl, combine the flour, oats, wheat germ, brown sugar, cinnamon, and salt. Add the apple juice concentrate and margarine. Blend with a fork or pastry blender until the mixture resembles coarse meal.

3. Pour two thirds of the crumb mixture into an 8-inch square baking pan that has been sprayed with nonstick vegetable coating and pack firmly. Bake for 15 minutes. Spoon the nectarine mixture over the baked layer and sprinkle the remaining crumbs on top. Bake until lightly browned, 25 to 30 minutes longer. Cool on a rack 15 minutes and then cut into bars. Serve warm or at room temperature.

MAKES 36 SERVINGS

Each serving contains approximately:
Calories / 68   Cholesterol / None
Fat / 3g   Sodium / 51mg

OATMEAL COOKIES

½ *pound (2 sticks) corn-oil margarine*
¾ *cup firmly packed brown sugar*
½ *cup sugar*
2 *large egg whites*
1 *teaspoon vanilla extract*
1½ *cups whole-wheat flour*
1 *teaspoon ground cinnamon*
1 *teaspoon baking soda*
1 *teaspoon baking powder*

¼ *teaspoon freshly grated nutmeg*
½ *teaspoon salt*
2½ *cups uncooked oatmeal, quick or old-fashioned*
½ *cup oat bran*

1. Preheat the oven to 375°F. Vigorously beat together the margarine and sugars in a large bowl until light and fluffy. Beat in the egg whites and vanilla until combined.

2. Combine the flour, cinnamon, baking soda, baking powder, nutmeg, and salt. Add to the margarine mixture, mixing well. Stir in the oats and oat bran.

3. Drop by rounded tablespoonsful onto an ungreased baking sheet. Bake until a light golden brown, 9 to 10 minutes. Remove to a wire cooling rack.

MAKES 4 DOZEN COOKIES

1 cookie contains approximately:
Calories / 95   *Cholesterol* / *None*
Fat / 5g   *Sodium* / 109mg

PEANUT BUTTER COOKIES

4 *tablespoons* (½ *stick*) *corn-oil margarine*
¾ *cup sugar*
¾ *cup firmly packed brown sugar*
1 *teaspoon vanilla extract*
1 *large egg plus 2 large egg whites, lightly beaten*
1½ *cups unbleached all-purpose flour*
1½ *cups whole-wheat flour*
2 *teaspoons baking soda*
Dash of salt
1 *cup unhomogenized peanut butter*

1. Preheat the oven to 375°F. In a food processor or with an electric mixer combine the margarine and sugars, mixing until light and fluffy. Add the vanilla, egg and egg whites and mix well.

2. Combine the dry ingredients in a medium-size bowl and add to the margarine mixture. Add the peanut butter and mix well. Drop by tablespoonsful on an ungreased baking sheet and flatten with a fork. Bake until golden brown, about 10 minutes.

MAKES 5½ DOZEN COOKIES

Each cookie contains approximately:
Calories / 138   Cholesterol / 8mg
Fat / 6g   Sodium / 82mg

SOFT PEANUT-BUTTER COOKIES

½ cup raisins
½ cup packed chopped dates
1 medium, ripe banana, mashed
⅓ cup unhomogenized creamy peanut butter
¼ cup water
2 large egg whites
1 teaspoon vanilla extract
1 cup old-fashioned oatmeal
½ cup whole-wheat flour
1 teaspoon baking soda

1. Preheat the oven to 350°F. In large mixing bowl combine the raisins, dates, banana, peanut butter, water, egg whites, and vanilla; beat until blended. Add the oatmeal, flour, and baking soda. Mix until thoroughly blended.

2. Drop by teaspoonsful onto a nonstick baking sheet. Bake until browned on the underside, about 10 minutes. Cool on a rack, then store in an airtight container.

MAKES ABOUT 50 COOKIES

Each cookie contains approximately:
Calories / 32   Cholesterol / None
Fat / 1g   Sodium / 17mg

DUNDEE DELIGHTS

⅔ cup corn-oil margarine
½ teaspoon salt
1½ teaspoons baking soda
1 teaspoon ground cinnamon
1 teaspoon ground allspice
1 cup sugar
3 large egg whites
2 cups old-fashioned oatmeal
½ cup chopped walnuts, toasted in a 350°F oven until
  golden brown, 8 to 10 minutes
½ cup raisins or chopped dried dates
3 cups unbleached all-purpose flour
6 tablespoons plain nonfat yogurt

1. Preheat the oven to 350°F. Using a spoon, combine the margarine, salt, baking soda, cinnamon, and allspice. Add the sugar and egg whites and mix well. Stir in the oatmeal, nuts, and raisins. Add the flour alternately with the yogurt.

2. Drop the dough by teaspoonsful onto an ungreased baking sheet and bake until the cookies are lightly browned, 12 to 15 minutes.

MAKES 6 DOZEN COOKIES

1 cookie contains approximately:
Calories / 62   Cholesterol / Negligible
Fat / 2g   Sodium / 57mg

LIGHTER GINGERSNAPS

⅓ cup corn-oil margarine
½ cup sugar
¼ cup liquid egg substitute or 2 large egg whites
¼ cup molasses
2 cups whole-wheat pastry flour
2 teaspoons baking soda
¼ teaspoon salt
1 teaspoon ground cinnamon
1 teaspoon ground cloves
½ teaspoon ground ginger
1 tablespoon sugar for sprinkling (optional)

1. Preheat the oven to 300°F. In a large mixing bowl, cream together the margarine and sugar. Add the egg substitute and molasses and mix well.

2. In a separate bowl, combine the flour, baking soda, salt, cinnamon, cloves, and ginger. Add the dry ingredients to the liquid ingredients and mix well.

3. Drop the dough by small rounded teaspoonsful on an ungreased baking sheet. If desired, sprinkle each cookie lightly with sugar. Bake for 15 minutes, then cool on a wire rack. Store in an airtight container.

MAKES ABOUT 36 COOKIES

Each cookie contains approximately:
Calories / 57   Cholesterol / None
Fat / 2g   Sodium / 65mg

APPLE AND CHEESE PLEASURES

¾ *cup unbleached all-purpose flour*
¼ *cup corn-oil margarine, at room temperature*
⅓ *cup firmly packed brown sugar*
¼ *cup liquid egg substitute*
1 *teaspoon vanilla extract*
½ *teaspoon ground cinnamon*
½ *teaspoon baking powder*
¼ *teaspoon salt*
1½ *cups old-fashioned oatmeal*
4 *ounces reduced-fat Cheddar cheese, shredded (1 cup)*
¾ *cup raisins*
1 *cup unsweetened applesauce*

1. Preheat the oven to 375°F. Combine the flour, margarine, sugar, egg substitute, vanilla, cinnamon, baking powder, and salt in large bowl and mix well. Add the oatmeal, cheese, and raisins and mix well. Stir in the applesauce, mixing well.

2. Drop by heaping tablespoonsful onto an ungreased baking sheet and bake until golden brown, 12 to 13 minutes. Cool on a rack and store in a tightly covered container in the refrigerator or in a loosely covered container at room temperature.

MAKES 24 COOKIES

Each cookie contains approximately:
Calories / 101   Cholesterol / 4mg
Fat / 3g   Sodium / 82mg

APPLE AND OATMEAL COOKIES

½ cup corn-oil margarine
½ cup firmly packed brown sugar
½ cup chopped walnuts, toasted in a 350°F oven until
  golden brown, 8 to 10 minutes
½ cup chopped raisins
1½ cups finely chopped, peeeled, and cored apple
¼ cup frozen unsweetened apple juice concentrate, thawed
1 teaspoon vanilla extract
3 large egg whites, lightly beaten
1½ cups whole-wheat flour
¾ cup old-fashioned oatmeal
½ teaspoon salt
2 teaspoons baking powder
1 teaspoon ground cinnamon

1. Preheat the oven to 350°F. Cream together the margarine and sugar in a large bowl. In a separate bowl, combine the remaining ingredients in the order listed, then stir into the creamed mixture.

3. Drop by teaspoonsful onto baking sheets that have been sprayed with nonstick vegetable coating and bake until golden, 12 to 16 minutes.

MAKES 3 TO 4 DOZEN COOKIES

Each cookie contains approximately:
Calories / 70   Cholesterol / None
Fat / 3g   Sodium / 95mg

BEVERAGES

Water is by far the healthiest beverage in the world, and it has finally come into its own as a status drink. You can now buy bottled water from almost every place in the world, plain or sparkling, flavored or natural, and with price tags ranging from nominal to outrageous. For anyone on a low-sodium diet, there are now many low-sodium soda waters available, as well as bottled distilled water, which is completely sodium-free.

There was a time when your guests would have been rather surprised, if not shocked, to have been offered water at a cocktail party. Now that it is the beverage of choice among many fitness-oriented young urban professionals, it is considered chic in many circles to serve a variety of waters at parties.

Water is also the basic ingredient for the most popular beverages, such as colas, coffee, and tea. Here we are seeing decaffeinated and caffeine-free varieties becoming much more popular and available. Caffeine is a drug that stimulates the adrenal glands to produce more adrenaline, which then acts as a stimulant, giving a false sense of energy.

Healthy alternatives to chocolate milk for children can be either carob milk or milk blended with old-fashioned unhomogenized peanut butter. Carob tastes a lot like chocolate, but it does not contain caffeine or saturated fat as chocolate does. Also it is naturally sweet so it doesn't need a lot of sugar and, being a plant, it contains fiber. It also has about four times the calcium found in chocolate or cocoa and none of the oxalic acid, which binds calcium and prevents absorption.

Also try "fruity" milk. Blend milk and fresh fruit such as peaches, strawberries, and bananas for after-school treats. For a quick milkshake, freeze sliced ripe bananas in plastic bags and then add them to a cup of skim milk and process until smooth. This is a good way to use up those bananas that are quickly becoming too ripe.

This section is short because so many recipes in this book can actually be turned into beverages simply by blending the ingredients with enough added liquid to make them easily drinkable. Many soups make good hot or cold beverages without any alteration.

It always amazes me when people tell me they are trying to lose weight by going on a liquid diet. *Liquid* certainly cannot be interpreted as low-calorie. There can be just as much nutrition in a liquid diet as in solid food. If you or anyone in your family is ever put on a liquid diet, simply blend up all of your favorite dishes and serve them in mugs!

FRESH FRUIT MILKSHAKE

*1 ripe banana or other fresh fruit, peeled and sliced (about
    ½ cup)*
¾ cup skim milk
Ground cinnamon or freshly grated nutmeg for garnish

1. Place the fruit in a tightly sealed plastic bag in the freezer
until the fruit is completely frozen. (This is an excellent way to
keep fruit from getting overripe.)

2. Combine the frozen fruit and milk in a blender and process until well blended and frothy. Pour in a glass and top with a
little ground cinnamon or freshly grated nutmeg.

MAKES 1 SERVING

Each serving contains approximately:
Calories / 170   Cholesterol / 3mg
Fat / 1g   Sodium / 95mg

BLUEBERRY SLUSH

1 cup frozen blueberries, unthawed
1 cup skim milk
1 tablespoon instant nonfat dry milk
1 tablespoon sugar

Combine all the ingredients in a blender and process on high
until smooth.

MAKES TWO ¾-CUP SERVINGS

Each serving contains approximately:
Calories / 115   Cholesterol / 2mg
Fat / 1g   Sodium / 77mg

PEANUT BUTTER FRAPPÉ

One 12-ounce can evaporated skimmed milk (1½ cups)
¼ cup unhomogenized peanut butter
2 tablespoons sugar
1 tablespoon vanilla extract
Dash of ground cinnamon
2 cups crushed ice

Combine all the ingredients in a blender and process on high until frothy.

MAKES FOUR 1-CUP SERVINGS

Each serving contains approximately:
Calories / 205   Cholesterol / 4mg
Fat / 8g   Sodium / 114mg

SPARKLING HONEYED LIMEADE

¾ cup fresh lime juice
¼ cup honey
3 cups sparkling water

Combine the lime juice and honey and mix until thoroughly blended. Add the sparkling water and mix well. Serve cold, poured over ice cubes.

MAKES FOUR 1-CUP SERVINGS

Each serving contains approximately:
Calories / 76   Cholesterol / None
Fat / Negligible   Sodium / 2mg

STRAWBERRY DAIQUIRI

2 cups unsweetened frozen strawberries, unthawed
2 tablespoons sugar
2 teaspoons rum extract
2 teaspoons fresh lemon juice
⅓ cup fresh orange juice
¾ cup crushed ice

Combine all the ingredients in a blender and process on high until frothy.

MAKES FOUR ¾-CUP SERVINGS

Each serving contains approximately:
Calories / 68   Cholesterol / None
Fat / Negligible   Sodium / 2mg

CAPPUCCINO

This recipe for Cappuccino mix and all of the following coffee mix recipes were designed as substitutes for the commercially packaged coffee mixes, which contain all sorts of additives that can't be pronounced and most certainly should be avoided when possible. Imitation vanilla butter and nut flavoring is an extract similar to vanilla and can be found in the same general area as the other extracts in your local supermarket under both the McCormick and the Schilling labels. If your local market doesn't carry it, ask your grocer to order it for you. It is a wonderful flavoring for all kinds of cakes and cookies because it imparts a slightly buttery flavor without the added fat.

4 teaspoons instant decaffeinated coffee granules
7 tablespoons plus 1½ teaspoons instant nonfat dry milk
4 teaspoons unsweetened cocoa powder
3 tablespoons plus 1 teaspoon granulated sugar
½ teaspoon imitation vanilla butter and nut flavoring or ¼
   teaspoon vanilla and ⅛ teaspoon almond extracts

1. Process all the ingredients in blender or food processor until well blended. Store, tightly covered, in the refrigerator.

2. To serve, put 1 level tablespoon of the mix in a mug or cup. Add ¾ cup boiling water and mix well.

MAKES ¾ CUP DRY MIX

1 tablespoon mix contains approximately:
Calories / 27   Cholesterol / 1mg
Fat / Negligible   Sodium / 19mg

VARIATION

Cappucino Amaretto: Add 1 teaspoon almond extract to above recipe before processing.

CAFÉ VIENNA

3 tablespoons instant decaffeinated coffee granules
7 tablespoons instant nonfat dry milk
3 tablespoons sugar
¼ teaspoon ground cinnamon
¼ teaspoon unsweetened cocoa powder
½ teaspoon imitation vanilla butter and nut flavoring or ¼
   teaspoon vanilla and ⅛ teaspoon almond extracts

1. Process all the ingredients in a blender or food processor until well blended.

2. To serve, put 1 level tablespoon of the mix in a mug or cup. Add ¾ cup boiling water and mix well.

MAKES ¾ CUP DRY MIX

1 tablespoon mix contains approximately:
Calories / 23   Cholesterol / 1mg
Fat / Negligible   Sodium / 15mg

CAFÉ FRANÇAISE

2 tablespoons instant decaffeinated coffee granules
11 tablespoons instant nonfat dry milk
1 tablespoon plus 2¼ teaspoons sugar
¾ teaspoon imitation vanilla butter and nut flavoring or ¼
*   teaspoon vanilla and ⅛ teaspoon almond extracts*

1. Process all the ingredients in a blender or food processor until well blended.

2. To serve, put 1 level tablespoon of the mix in a mug or cup. Add ¾ cup boiling water and mix well.

MAKES ¾ CUP DRY MIX

1 tablespoon mix contains approximately:
Calories / 22   Cholesterol / 1mg
Fat / Negligible   Sodium / 22mg

SWISS MOCHA

---

2 tablespoons unsweetened cocoa powder
2 tablespoons instant decaffeinated coffee granules
5 tablespoons instant nonfat dry milk
2 tablespoons sugar or to taste
¼ teaspoon vanilla extract

1. Process all the ingredients in a blender or food processor until well blended.

2. To serve, put 1 level tablespoon of the mix in a mug or cup. Add ¾ cup boiling water and mix well.

MAKES ¾ CUP DRY MIX

1 tablespoon mix contains approximately:
Calories / 28   Cholesterol / Negligible
Fat / Negligible   Sodium / 18mg

INDEX

CONTENTS